Origami Buch für Beginner 3

Lerne wunderschöne Origami-Figuren zu erstellen Schritt für Schritt für Kinder und Erwachsene

© Copyright - Alle Rechte vorbehalten.

Der in diesem Buch enthaltene Inhalt darf nicht reproduziert, vervielfältigt oder übertragen werden ohne direkte schriftliche Erlaubnis des Autors oder des Herausgebers reproduziert, vervielfältigt oder übertragen werden.

Unter keinen Umständen wird irgendeine Schuld oder rechtliche Verantwortung gegenüber dem Herausgeber oder dem Autor, für für Schäden, Wiedergutmachung oder finanzielle Verluste aufgrund der Informationen, die in diesem Buch enthalten sind, weder direkt noch indirekt.

Rechtlicher Hinweis:

Dieses Buch ist urheberrechtlich geschützt. Es ist nur für den persönlichen Gebrauch bestimmt. Sie dürfen es nicht verändern, verteilen, verkaufen, verwenden, zitieren oder den Inhalt dieses Buches ohne die Zustimmung des Autors oder die Zustimmung des Autors oder Herausgebers.

Hinweis zum Haftungsausschluss:

Bitte beachten Sie, dass die in diesem Dokument enthaltenen Informationen nur zu Bildungsund Unterhaltungszwecken dienen. Es wurden alle Anstrengungen unternommen, um genaue, aktuelle, zuverlässige und vollständige Informationen zu präsentieren. Es werden keine Garantien jeglicher Art gegeben oder impliziert. Der Leser nimmt zur Kenntnis, dass der Autor nicht tätig ist in einer rechtlichen, finanziellen, medizinischen oder professionelle Beratung. Der Inhalt dieses Buches wurde aus verschiedenen Quellen entnommen. Bitte konsultieren Sie einen lizenzierten Fachmann, bevor Sie die in diesem Buch beschriebenen Techniken ausprobieren.

Durch das Lesen dieses Dokuments erklärt sich der Leser damit einverstanden, dass der Autor unter keinen Umständen für irgendwelche Verluste, direkt oder indirekt, verantwortlich ist, die infolge der Verwendung der in diesem Dokument enthaltenen Informationen entstanden sind, einschließlich, aber nicht beschränkt auf, Fehler, Auslassungen oder Ungenauigkeiten.

Inhaltsverzeichnis

Einführung 6
   Was ist Origami? 6
   Eine kurze Geschichte von Origami 7
   Papierfalten in Europa 9
   Modernes Origami 10
   Symbolik in Origami 13
      Schachteln und Umschläge *13*
      Samurai-Helm *13*
      Tsuru *14*
      Tatsu *14*
      Neko *15*
      Kaeru *15*
      Chocho *16*
Symbole 17
Falttechniken 18
Modell-Liste 19

Elefant *22*
Eule *25*
Frosch *28*
Schlange *32*
Blatt *34*
Schwäne *38*
Garnele *42*
Affe *46*
Ente *51*

Lilie *54*

Pinguin *57*

Güteltier *61*

Krebs *65*

Schnecke *69*

Krokodil *73*

Vogel *79*

Einleitung

Origami ist eine alte Kunstform mit einer Geschichte, die so alt und reichhaltig wie das Papier, aus dem es gemacht ist. Als sich das Papier entwickelte und verfeinert wurde, entwickelte sich auch die Origami-Kunst, und sie wurde immer beliebter und verbreitete sich über die ganze Welt. Während Kulturen überall auf der Welt ihre eigenen Formen der Papierfaltkunst haben, ist die japanische Origami-Kunst die Kunstform, die am beliebtesten geworden ist und die Welt im Sturm erobert hat.

Origami kann so einfach oder komplex sein, wie es sich der Künstler wünscht. Designs wie ein schlichtes, einfaches Herz oder ein Hund können eine großartige Einführung in diese Kunst für Kinder sein, um sich danach, mit erweiterten Fähigkeiten, an komplexere Figuren zu wagen, wie einen Kranich oder ein Nashorn aus Papier. Engagierte Künstler können lernen, wunderschöne Meisterwerke zu formen, wie z. B. einen verschlungenen chinesischer Drache mit individuellen Schuppen, die alle aus einem einem einzigen Stück Papier gefaltet. Dies ist eine großartige Kunst zu lernen, da die Leichtigkeit, mit der Sie beginnen großartig für Anfänger geeignet ist. Ganz zu schweigen davon, dass es eine der erschwinglichsten Kunstformen ist, die es gibt, denn selbst wenn Sie kein richtiges Origamipapier in die Hände bekommen, können Sie mit jedem Papier, das Sie zu Hause oder im Büro herumliegen haben, eine Menge Übung machen.

Origami ist eine wunderbare Kunstform, und wenn Sie ein wenig mehr darüber wissen, woher sie kommt, können Sie sie auf einer tieferen Ebene schätzen.

Was ist Origami?

In Wahrheit sagt der Name bereits alles. Das Wort Origami setzt sich aus zwei japanischen Wörtern zusammen: „oru", was übersetzt „falten" bedeutet, und „kami", was übersetzt „Papier" bedeutet. Origami ist also die Kunst, Tiere, Blumen, Figuren, Schachteln, Bäume usw. aus Papier zu falten. Ein wichtiges Element des Origami ist, dass das Papier in keiner Weise geschnitten oder gerissen wird. Das Papier kann auch nicht geklebt oder mit Klebeband fixiert werden, um Kanten oder Ecken an ihrem Platz zu halten.

Stattdessen werden geschickte Faltungen und Knicke verwendet, um dies zu erreichen. Traditionell wird jede Origami-Figur mit einem einzigen Stück Papier gefaltet, aber modernere Designs haben Möglichkeiten eingebaut, zwei oder drei Stücke für ein größeres Projekt zusammenzufalten. Es ist auch traditionell, keine Markierungen mit einem Stift oder Bleistift auf dem Origami zu machen, entweder um Faltlinien zu markieren oder als Dekoration. Echtes Origamipapier hat auch eine leere und eine farbige Seite, aber Sie können trotzdem jedes beliebige Papier verwenden, solange es Ihren Bedürfnissen entspricht.

Kurze Geschichte des Origami

Der genaue Ursprung des Papierfaltens als Kunstform ist im Allgemeinen nicht sicher, und viele glauben, dass die Ursprünge älter sind als das Papier selbst, als dekorative Falttechniken auf andere biegsame Materialien wie Seide und Leder angewendet wurden. Als Papier im Jahr 105 n. Chr. in China entstand, entdeckte man, dass es das perfekte Material zum Falten war: lockerer und flexibler als Leder und daher zu viel feineren Details fähig, aber stabiler als Seide und in der Lage, seine Form viel besser zu halten. Irgendwann zwischen dem sechsten und siebten Jahrhundert wurde diese Kunst nach Japan gebracht und die Saat des Origami war gelegt. Damals als Origata bekannt, war die Kunst des Papierfaltens aufgrund der Seltenheit des Papiers ein exklusives Ritual, das von den Samurai und heiligen Männern und Frauen ausgeführt wurde. Als Bestandteil von Shintō-Ritualen wurden dekorative Schachteln und Umschläge aus Papier gefaltet und zum Einpacken von Opfergaben an die Götter verwendet. Es wurde auch populär, Origata zu verwenden, um Verlobungsund Hochzeitsgeschenke zu überreichen.

In der Edo-Periode, von 1603 bis 1868, wurde handgeschöpftes Washi-Papier leichter verfügbar und ermöglichte es, dass das Papierfalten zu einem beliebten Hobby der einfachen Leute wurde, sowohl für Erwachsene als auch für Kinder. Diese „gewöhnlichere" und weniger ritualisierte Form des Papierfaltens wurde als Origami bekannt. Abgesehen davon, dass es eine lustige Art war, sich die Zeit zu vertreiben, nutzten die einfachen Leute Origami als billige und einfache Möglichkeit, ihre Häuser und Geschenke zu dekorieren.

Wie bei den meisten Elementen der japanischen Kunst war es üblich, Origami-Figuren zu falten, die Elementen der Natur ähnelten, wie zum Beispiel Tiere, Pflanzen und sogar Blumenmuster. Origami wurde in dieser Zeit so populär, dass es in andere Formen der Kunst integriert wurde, und es gab sogar ganze Gemälde, die Frauen beim Falten von Origami in ihren Häusern zeigten.

Ursprünglich waren die gefalteten Figuren recht einfach und leicht, aber als die Kunst geübt wurde, wurden mehr Techniken und kompliziertere Designs entdeckt und weitergegeben. In dieser Zeit entwickelte sich die Kunst zu einer Tradition und einem Teil der Kultur mit einer tieferen Bedeutung. Die kulturelle Bedeutung, die mit bestimmten Tieren und anderen Symbolen und Figuren verbunden war, wurde auf ihre Origami-Gegenstücke übertragen, und sogar verschiedene Arten von Faltungen erhielten eine gewisse Bedeutung. Im Jahr 1797 wurde ein Buch mit dem Titel Hiden Senbazuru Origata oder Das Geheimnis des Faltens von 1000 Papierkranichen von Akisato Rito veröffentlicht, in dem er die kulturelle Bedeutung der Kunst erklärt und 49 verschiedene Arten des Faltens von Papierkranichen vorstellt. Dies war die erste schriftliche Aufzeichnung dieser Kunst.

Im Jahr 1954 wurde die traditionelle Origami-Kunst revolutioniert, als Akira Yoshizawa ein Buch mit dem Titel Atarashi Origami Geijutsu veröffentlichte, was übersetzt Die neue Origami-Kunst bedeutet.

In diesem Buch stellte der Autor nicht nur das Konzept vor, Origami als pädagogisches Hilfsmittel zu verwenden, um Kindern bestimmte grundlegende mathematische Konzepte beizubringen, sondern er verwendete auch neue Muster, die Origami-Künstler dazu ermutigten, das Papier zu schneiden, zu reißen, zu befeuchten und zu kleben, um komplizierte neue Figuren zu schaffen. Mit diesen neuen Origami-Designs waren die Künstler nicht mehr darauf beschränkt, nur ein quadratisches Stück Papier zu verwenden, und die Kunstform erfreute sich einer neuen Welle der Popularität. Dieses Buch trug auch dazu bei, die Kunstform im Rest der Welt zu verbreiten und die japanische Kunst des Papierfaltens zu einer weltweiten Sensation zu machen.

Papierfalten in Europa

Auf der anderen Seite der Welt wurde eine andere Form des Papierfaltens geboren. Es wird angenommen, dass es zwei Hauptursprünge dieser Kunst in Europa gibt. Der erste ist eine Reihe von geometrischen, mathematischen Formen des Faltens. Diese spezifischen Muster wurden von den Mauren in Spanien eingeführt. Die Spanier nahmen dieses neue Konzept sehr gut auf und entwickelten daraus ihre eigene, einzigartige Kunstform, die pajarita.

Ein anderer europäischer Ursprung des Papierfaltens hat mehr Ähnlichkeiten mit dem japanischen Origami, da es ebenfalls aus einer anderen Form der Faltkunst entwickelt wurde. Im frühen siebzehnten Jahrhundert war es äußerst beliebt, Servietten zu komplizierten geometrischen Mustern und dreidimensionalen Figuren zu falten. Dies war vor allem bei Adeligen und Wohlhabenden beliebt, die diese Serviettenfalttechniken nutzten, um Gäste bei Feiern oder Dinnerpartys zu beeindrucken. Während dieser Zeit war es in den wohlhabenderen Familien nicht ungewöhnlich, einige dieser Falttechniken auf Papier anzuwenden, aber dies wurde eher als ein lustiges Hobby oder Zeitvertreib angesehen als ein echtes Handwerk oder eine Kunstform.

Erst im neunzehnten Jahrhundert wurde das Papierfalten populär, nachdem ein Mann namens Friedrich Fröbel das Konzept in die Kindergärten brachte. Eine der Freizeitund Bildungsaktivitäten im Lehrplan war das Papierfalten, bei dem Serviettenfalttechniken angewendet wurden, um den Kindern zu helfen, niedliche, lustige Figuren zu falten. Als die Kinder ihren Eltern zeigten, was sie gelernt hatten, weckte das auch das Interesse der Erwachsenen. Als diese neue Art des Serviettenfaltens immer beliebter wurde und sich in ganz Europa verbreitete, wurden neue Techniken angewandt, und das Papierfalten entwickelte sich zu einer eigenen Kunstform. Als sich europäische und japanische Kulturen trafen und begannen, miteinander zu interagieren, wurden Serviettenund Papierfalttechniken ausgetauscht und die Kunst wurde noch interessanter und vielfältiger.

Modernes Origami

Das moderne Origami, das wir heute kennen, hat einige signifikante Unterschiede zu der Kunstform, die während der Edo-Zeit praktiziert wurde.

An erster Stelle steht die Tatsache, dass derjenige, der neue Origami-Faltfolgen kreiert, Anerkennung erhält. Traditionell wurden Origami-Techniken und -Sequenzen mündlich von Generation zu Generation weitergegeben, etwa indem eine Frau ihren Kindern und deren Freunden eine Origami-Sequenz beibrachte, die sie von ihrer eigenen Mutter gelernt hatte. Wenn neue Faltfolgen entstanden, wurden sie anonym in der Gemeinschaft eingeführt. Ein Beispiel: Eine junge Frau kreiert eine neue Sequenz und zeigt sie ihren Freunden. Alle diese Freunde zeigen diese neue Sequenz dann ihren Freunden, und so weiter, bis das ganze Dorf die neue Sequenz gelernt hat und sich niemand mehr so recht erinnern kann, woher sie stammt. So blieben die genialen Schöpfer dieser Techniken und Sequenzen der Geschichte unbekannt, und niemand kann eine Sequenz zu ihrem Ursprungsort zurückverfolgen.

Dies änderte sich im 20. Jahrhundert, als ein Sōtō-Priester als erster Mensch überhaupt eine Origami-Sequenz registrieren und patentieren ließ und damit die Anerkennung für seine neue Schöpfung beanspruchte. Dieser monumentale Akt inspirierte einen neuen Glauben, dass diejenigen mit dem Intellekt und der Kunstfertigkeit, neue Sequenzen zu schaffen, die gebührende Anerkennung für ihre Fähigkeiten erhalten sollten. Das bedeutete, dass mehr und mehr Künstler begannen, ihre Arbeit zu patentieren, und neue Origami-Sequenzen wurden sogar urheberrechtlich geschützt. Dies machte Origami zu einer viel persönlicheren Form der Kunst. Zusammen mit der begrenzten Möglichkeit, eine Sequenz mündlich zu lehren, schuf dieses Format auch ein Problem mit der Zugänglichkeit. Wenn man eine bestimmte Origami-Sequenz lernen wollte, musste man jemanden finden, der wusste, wie man sie faltet, und ihn dann überzeugen, sie einem beizubringen. Aus diesem Grund blieben die Sequenzen in der Regel innerhalb der Familien oder Gemeinschaften, in denen sie entstanden, und obwohl es einige gab, die Anleitungen für ihre Sequenzen aufschrieben, hatte jeder seine eigene Art, es zu tun, und die Sprache blieb eine Barriere.

In den 1930er Jahren entwickelte ein Mann namens Akira Yoshizawa ein System zur Dokumentation von Faltfolgen durch die Verwendung von Diagrammen, Linien und Pfeilen. Dieses Diagrammsystem war leicht zu verstehen und hatte nicht die Einschränkungen, die die Sprachbarrieren mit sich brachten, und zwanzig Jahre später begannen die Origami-Faltsequenzen weltweit unter Verwendung dieses Systems veröffentlicht zu werden. Diese neue Verfügbarkeit und der einfache Zugang zu den Sequenzen trugen wesentlich zu dem neuen Popularitätsschub bei, den die Origami-Kunst in der modernen Gesellschaft erfahren hat. Ein weiterer wesentlicher Unterschied zwischen traditionellem und modernem Origami ist die Freiheit in der Anwendung und Nutzung des Origami. Mit der Veröffentlichung von The New Origami Art und den neuen Techniken, die durch verschiedene Kulturen eingeführt wurden, wurde den Origami-Künstlern viel mehr Freiheit zugestanden. Sie konnten ihr Papier so modifizieren, dass es besser zu ihren Entwürfen passte, und eine ganze Welle neuer Origami-Kreationen wurde in die Welt hinausgelassen, sowohl für diejenigen, die Origami als Hobby praktizieren, als auch für diejenigen, die die Kunst in professionellen Kreisen verfolgen. Den Künstlern wurde erlaubt, viel kompliziertere und stabilere Designs und Faltfolgen zu kreieren. Selbst diejenigen, die den traditionellen Methoden folgen und ein einziges Stück Papier verwenden, sind zu viel fortschrittlicheren und komplexeren Techniken fähig als das, was in der Vergangenheit möglich war. Komplexe mathematische Gleichungen werden oft verwendet, um das Papier in bestimmten Bereichen vor dem Falten zu falten, um tiefere Dimensionen, realistischere Modelle und kompliziertere Faltfolgen zu schaffen, was eine ganz neue Ebene der Kunstfertigkeit in die wunderbare Kunst des Origami bringt.

Der letzte bedeutende Unterschied ist der Zweck von Origami. Die Tradition, Origami und Origata für bestimmte Rituale zu verwenden, lebt immer noch weiter. Während Origami immer noch am häufigsten als lustiger Zeitvertreib verwendet wird, um interessante Dekorationen und Geschenke zu machen, hat sich diese Kunst zu viel mehr als das entwickelt. Mit der Anerkennung von Künstlern für ihre Kreationen werden großartige Origami-Kunstwerke als künstlerische Errungenschaften gewürdigt und sind in Kunstausstellungen und Galerien weltweit zu finden.

Es werden sogar neue Faltfolgen speziell für den Zweck geschaffen, große Kunstwerke zu konstruieren. Auch die Situationen, in denen man Origami verschenkt, haben sich stark verändert. Ursprünglich wurden Origami-Geschenke zu bestimmten Anlässen wie religiösen Zeremonien, Hochzeiten und Beerdigungen überreicht, bei denen das Geschenk eine bestimmte kulturelle oder spirituelle Bedeutung hatte. Dieser Brauch besteht zwar immer noch, aber Origami-Geschenke sind inzwischen viel verbreiteter, und man kann einem Freund ein süßes kleines Papiertier schenken, einfach weil einem danach ist. In der heutigen Zeit ist der Hauptzweck eines Origami-Geschenkes, Ihre neue Kunst mit anderen zu teilen und jemandem zu zeigen, dass Sie sich genug um ihn kümmern, um Zeit und Mühe in die Herstellung von etwas für ihn zu investieren, anstatt einfach etwas zu kaufen. Origami ist auch eine schöne Art, Geschenke zu überreichen, wie z.B. das Falten von Blumen, um sie auf eine Karte zu legen, Schachteln, um Geschenke darin zu verstauen, oder einfache Objekte, die eine liebevolle Botschaft offenbaren, wenn man sie auffaltet. Es ist auch populär geworden, Origami mit Papierscheinen als eine clevere, kreative Art, jemandem Geld zu schenken, zu verwenden.

Auch die Popkultur und die moderne Technologie haben ihre Spuren im modernen Origami hinterlassen. Mit Computern und dem Internet ist es einfacher als je zuvor, eine Origami-Sequenz in die Hände zu bekommen, und auch das Erstellen und Teilen neuer Diagramme ist ein Kinderspiel. Dies, zusammen mit der Tatsache, dass es eine erschwingliche Kunstform ist, ist einer der Hauptgründe, warum Origami heute so unglaublich beliebt ist. Ein weiterer Grund, warum Origami so beliebt ist, ist die Tatsache, dass es in allen beliebten Filmen, Serien, Animes und Büchern verwendet wurde. Es wird nicht schwierig sein, Anleitungen zu finden, wie Sie Ihre Lieblingsfilmfigur oderikone aus Papier falten können.

Symbolik im Origami

In der heutigen Zeit hat nicht mehr jedes einzelne Stück Origami und jede Falte eine tiefere Bedeutung oder Symbolik als früher, aber es gibt einige alte, traditionelle Origami-Figuren, die immer noch die kulturelle Bedeutung haben, die sie einst während der Edo-Zeit hatten. Diese werden oft als Geschenk mit einem bestimmten Zweck und einer bestimmten Symbolik verschenkt.

Schachteln und Umschläge

Obwohl dekorative Schachteln und Umschläge, die aus Papier gefaltet werden, nicht unbedingt auf Geschenke und Hochzeitsgeschenke beschränkt sind, ist es immer noch ein beliebter Brauch, selbst Schachteln zu basteln, um kleine Geschenke zu überreichen und so zu zeigen, dass man sich um den Empfänger kümmert und dass er etwas Besonderes für einen ist. Besonders beliebt ist es, diese handgemachten Geschenke an Freunde, Familie und Angehörige zu verschenken.

Samurai-Helm

Samurai sind in der japanischen Kultur das, was Ritter in glänzender Rüstung in unserer sind. Sie sind wilde, tapfere Krieger, die für das Königreich kämpfen und böse Bestien erschlagen. Die Samurai stehen für Mut und Ritterlichkeit und natürlich für Männlichkeit - jeder Junge träumt davon, irgendwann in seiner Jugend ein Samurai zu werden. Ein Origami-Samurai-Helm trägt etwas von dieser Symbolik in sich und ist zu einem der häufigsten Symbole für den 5. Mai geworden, der in Japan als „Boy's Day" oder „Children's Day" gefeiert wird. Dieser Feiertag feiert die gesunde Geburt und das Wachstum von Kindern, insbesondere von Jungen. Während dieses Feiertags werden Häuser und Gebäude oft mit Origami-Samurai-Helmen geschmückt. Ein anderer beliebter Brauch an diesem Tag ist es, einen großen Helm aus Zeitungspapier zu falten, den ein Kind den ganzen Tag über tragen kann.

Tsuru

Der Kranich ist wahrscheinlich die ikonischste Origami-Figur der Welt, auch wenn es sich um eine ziemlich komplizierte Sequenz handelt. In der japanischen Kultur ist der Kranich ein majestätisches Symbol für Frieden, Treue und Langlebigkeit. Diese Symbolik hat sich in vielerlei Hinsicht auf die Papierform dieses Vogels übertragen. Der Kranich wird oft gefaltet und als Gebet für den Frieden verschenkt. Aufgrund seiner Assoziation mit langem Leben wird er auch als Symbol für Gesundheit verwendet und wird oft an Kranke oder Verletzte verschenkt, um ihnen zu wünschen, dass sie bald wieder gesund werden.

Um den Papierkranich rankt sich auch eine sehr interessante Legende: Es wird geglaubt, dass wenn man es schafft, 1.000 Kraniche zu falten, sein einziger, tiefster Wunsch erfüllt wird. Aufgrund dieses Glaubens und der Assoziation mit Gesundheit und langem Leben ist es zu einem Brauch geworden, einen senbazuru zu machen. Ein Senbazuru wird hergestellt, indem man 1.000 Kraniche faltet und sie mit Schnüren zusammenbindet. Diese Kranichschnüre werden dann an Menschen verschenkt, die schwer krank sind oder eine Naturkatastrophe erlitten haben. Es ist nicht ungewöhnlich, ein oder zwei senbazuru zu sehen, wenn man ein Krankenhaus in Japan besucht. Der Senbazuru steht auch für einen großen Wunsch nach Frieden in der Welt.

Tatsu

Drachen sind in der chinesischen, japanischen und vietnamesischen Kultur seit langem ein Symbol der Macht, und obwohl östliche Drachen ganz anders aussehen als die, die wir kennen, gibt es Origami-Sequenzen, um beide Arten zu falten. Origami-Drachen werden normalerweise gefaltet, um großes Glück und Erfolg in Ihr Leben einzuladen, und sie können auch als ein Weg geschaffen werden, um emotionale Stärke während schwieriger Zeiten anzufordern. Origami-Drachen werden auch verschenkt, wenn jemand etwas Neues beginnt oder einen wichtigen Schritt im Leben macht - wie z.B. einen neuen Job antritt, in ein neues Haus zieht oder eine wichtige Prüfung ablegt - und man ihm viel Glück wünschen möchte. Origami-Drachen können auch verschenkt oder an einem Geschenk befestigt werden, um jemandem Erfolg und Glück im Leben im Allgemeinen zu wünschen.

Neko

Katzen sind seit jeher ein wichtiger Teil der japanischen Kultur und stehen für Unabhängigkeit, Weisheit und Geheimnisse und sind seit langem ein Symbol für Glück. Es wird geglaubt, dass Katzen großes Glück bringen können, besonders wenn es um Geschäfte geht, und in gewisser Weise werden Katzen mit finanziellem Wohlstand in Verbindung gebracht. Katzen sind ein so hervorragender Glücksbringer, dass eine Katzenfigur mit einer winkenden Pfote, auch bekannt als Maneki-Neko, zu einem Must-Have für Unternehmen in ganz Japan und China geworden ist. Diese winkende Katze findet man an den Eingängen von Restaurants, Geschäften und sogar in den Büros von kleinen Unternehmen, um Glück zu bringen und gute Geschäfte einzuladen. Eine Origami-Katze zu falten und sie bei sich zu tragen, kann eine großartige Möglichkeit sein, Glück und finanziellen Erfolg in Ihr Leben einzuladen. Es gibt Dutzende von Faltfolgen für Origami-Katzen, und Sie können sogar lernen, wie man speziell eine Maneki-Neko faltet.

Kaeru

Das japanische Wort für „Frosch" ist auch das japanische Wort für „Rückkehr". Der Frosch ist also ein spirituelles Symbol für die Rückkehr des Verlorenen. Origami-Frösche werden oft gefaltet und verschenkt, um dieses Konzept der Rückgabe von Dingen zu fördern. Der häufigste Brauch ist es, einen kleinen Origami-Frosch in der Brieftasche oder im Geldbeutel zu tragen, in der Hoffnung, dass man das Geld, das man ausgeben will, bald zurückerhält. So steht der Frosch für solide Investitionen und Weisheit in finanziellen Angelegenheiten. Wenn Sie die ultimative finanzielle Hilfe wollen, sollten Sie immer eine Origami-Katze und einen Frosch zusammen bei sich tragen, wobei die Katze das Glück und den Reichtum einlädt und der Frosch dafür sorgt, dass Sie beim Ausgeben dieses Reichtums weise arbeiten.

Ein anderer beliebter Brauch ist es, Origami-Frösche an Menschen zu verschenken, um deren Rückkehr zu sichern. Wenn jemand auf eine Reise geht, wird ihm ein Frosch geschenkt, um ihm eine sichere Reise und eine sichere Rückkehr zu wünschen. Wenn ein Kind aus dem Haus zieht oder ein Freund oder Familienmitglied weit weg zieht, ermutigt der geschenkte Frosch sie, ihn bald und oft zu besuchen.

Chocho

Schmetterlinge haben in verschiedenen Kulturen sowohl positive als auch negative Assoziationen, aber in der japanischen Kultur haben sie eine sehr schöne Bedeutung. Ein Schmetterling repräsentiert all die Hoffnungen und Wünsche eines jungen Mädchens beim Übergang in die Weiblichkeit.

In der japanischen Kultur falten junge Mädchen oft Origami-Schmetterlinge, um diese Hoffnungen und Träume irgendwie auszudrücken und festzuhalten.

Zwei Schmetterlinge zusammen tragen eine neue Bedeutung und repräsentieren eine glückliche, glückselige Ehe. Aus diesem Grund werden Papierschmetterlinge oft als Dekoration bei Hochzeiten verwendet, und es ist ein beliebter Brauch, alle Geschenke, die dem Brautpaar überreicht werden, mit einem schönen Origami-Schmetterlingspaar zu verzieren.

Symbole

Lines

——————— Kantenlinie. Zeigt die Papierkante.

——————— Geknickte Linie. Zeigt die Falzlinie vom vorherigen Schritt.

– – – – – – – Talfaltenlinie. Zeigt die Falz, wenn die Papierkante nach unten zeigt.

–·–·–·–·–·–·– Berg-Falzlinie. Zeig den Falz, wenn die Papierkante nach oben zeigt.

················· Imaginäre Linie. Zeigt die Papierposition, nachdem der Schritt ausgeführt wurde.

Arrows

 Richtungspfeil. Zeigt die Richtung an, in die das Papier gefaltet werden soll.

 Pfeil zum Falten und Entfalten. Zeigt an, dass nur Falzlinie gemacht werden muss.

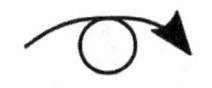 Pfeil zum Wenden. Zeigt an, dass Modell für weitere Schritte umgedreht werden soll.

 Quetschpfeil. Zeigt an, dass das Papier nach unten gedrückt werden muss.

 Pfeil zum Drehen. Zeigt die Richtung an, in die das Modell gedreht werden soll.

Falten

Talfalte

 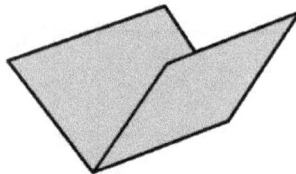

Falten Sie die Seiten nach oben und lassen Sie dabei die Faltkante nach unten gehen. Das Papier bildet eine Figur, ähnlich einem Tal.

Bergfalte

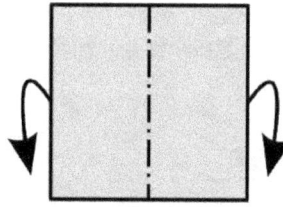 

Falten Sie die Seiten nach unten und lassen Sie die Faltkante nach oben gehen. Das Papier bildet eine Figur, die einem Berg ähnelt.

Quetschfalte

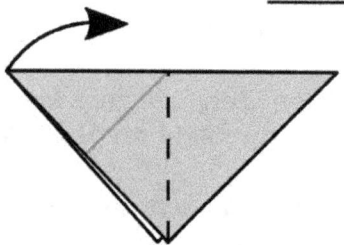 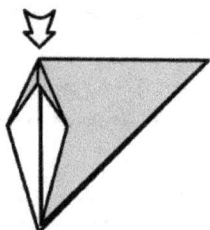 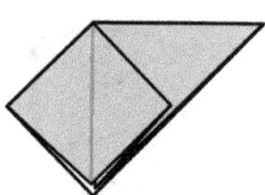

Falten in zwei Stufen. Zuerst wird die Ecke senkrecht nach oben gefaltet und dann wird sie mit Hilfe von bereits vorgefertigten Linien nach unten gedrückt.

Modell Liste

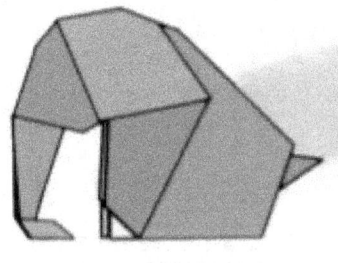

Seite 22-24

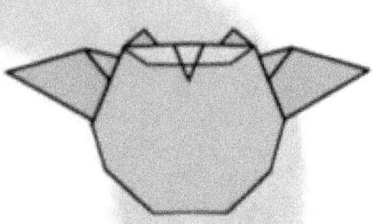

Seite 25-27

Seite 28-31

Seite 32-33

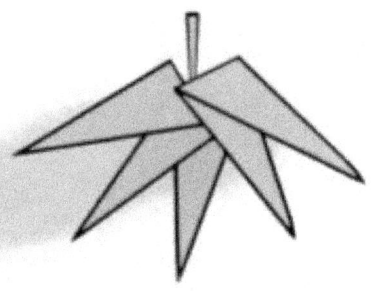

Seite 34-37

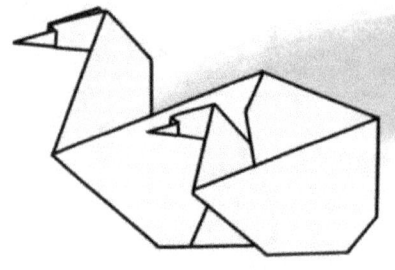
Seite 38-41

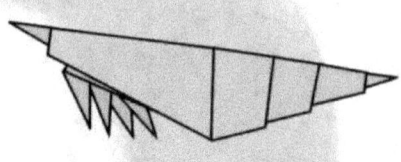
Seite 42-45

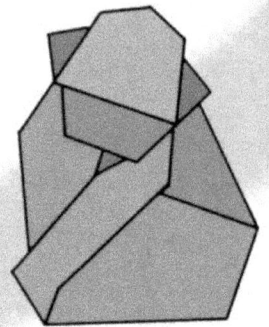
Seite 46-50

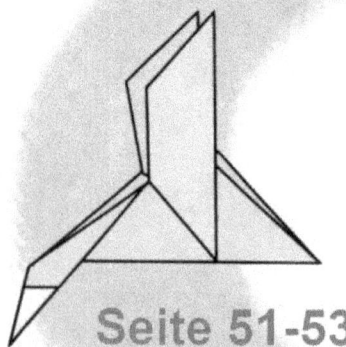
Seite 51-53

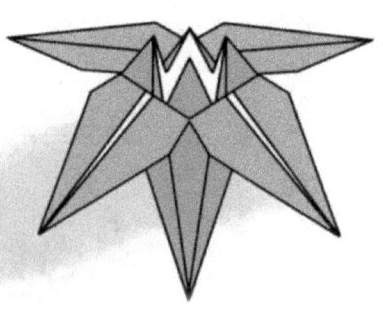
Seite 54-56

Seite 57-60

Seite 61-64

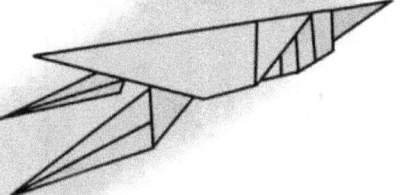
Seite 65-68

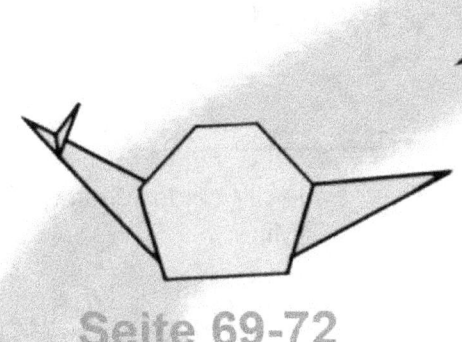
Seite 69-72

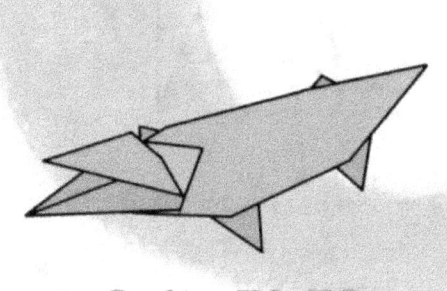
Seite 73-78

Seite 79-81

Elefant

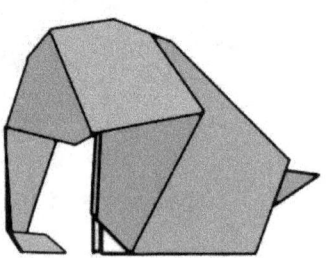
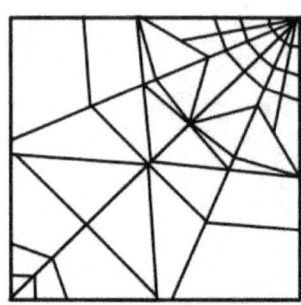

1 Beginne mit der weißen Seite nach oben.

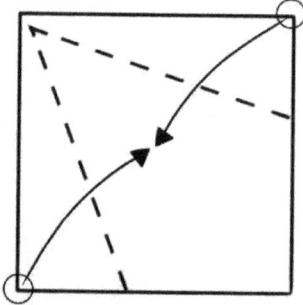

2 Falte die beiden Seiten zur Mitte.

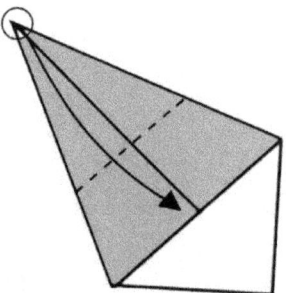

3 Falte nach unten.

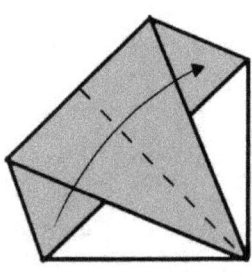

4 In der Hälfte falten.

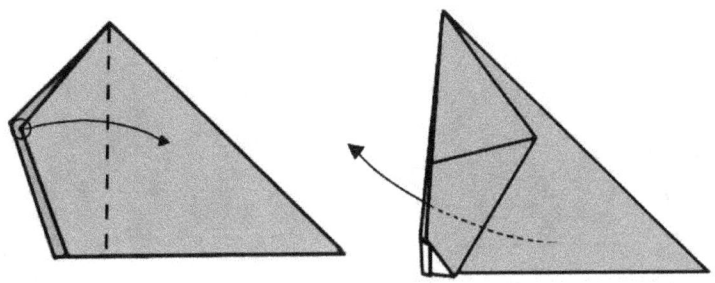

5 Falte die beiden Seiten an den gestrichelten Linien.

6 Ziehe die innere Lage heraus.

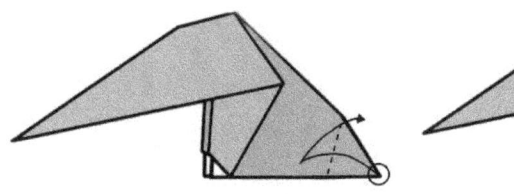

7 Falt die Tasche und entfalte, um den Schwanz zu bilden.

8 Mache eine Stufenfaltung.

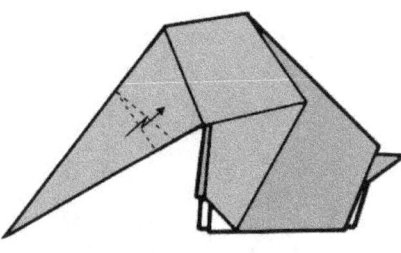
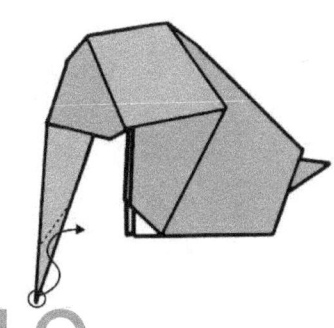

9 Mache erneut eine Stufenfaltung.

10 Taschenfalte.

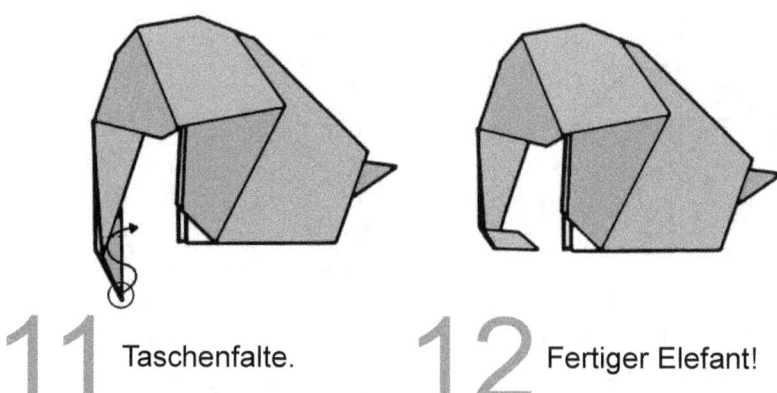

11 Taschenfalte. **12** Fertiger Elefant!

Eule

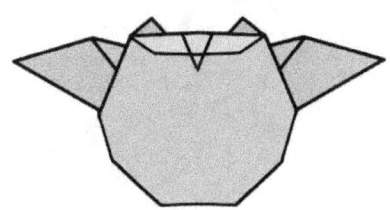
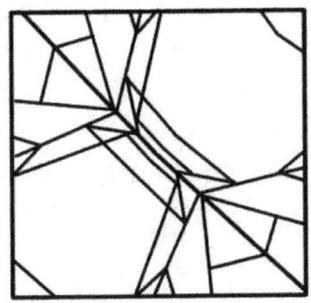

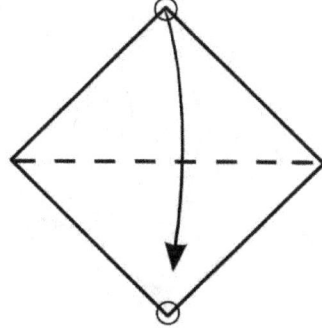

1 Beginne mit der weißen Seite nach oben.

2 Falte diagonal in der Hälfte.

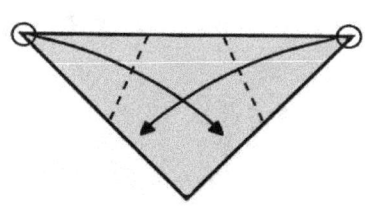
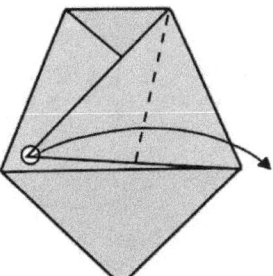

3 Falte die beiden Seiten an den gestrichelten Linien.

4 Falte bis zum markierten Punkt.

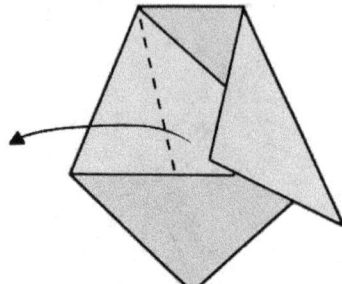 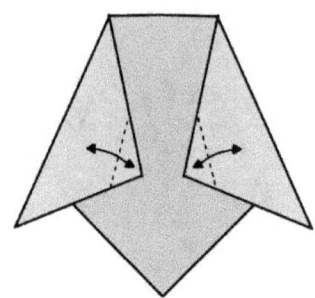

5 Falte die Flügel an der gestrichelten Linie.

6 Falte und entfalte an den gestrichelten Linien.

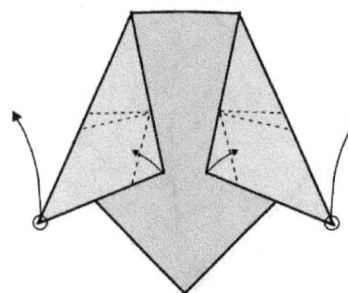 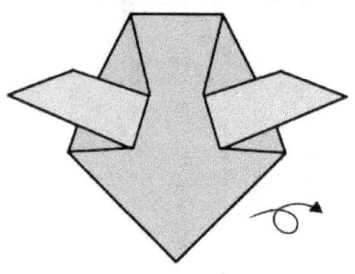

7 Falte die Flügel diagonal nach oben. Klappe untere Punkte nach innen.

8 Drehe das Modell um.

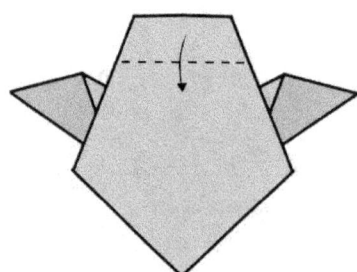 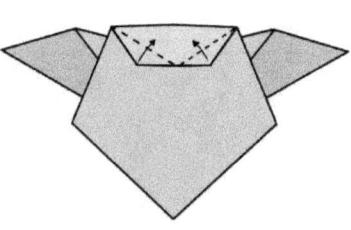

9 Nach unten falten.

10 Nach innen falten.

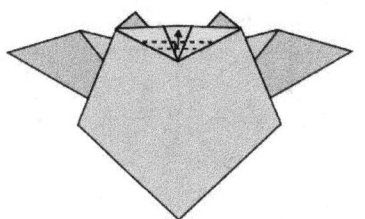

11 Mach eine Stufenfaltung.

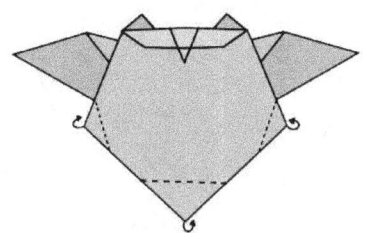

12 Falte die Ecken nach innen.

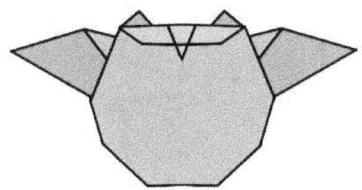

13 Fertige Eule!

Frosch

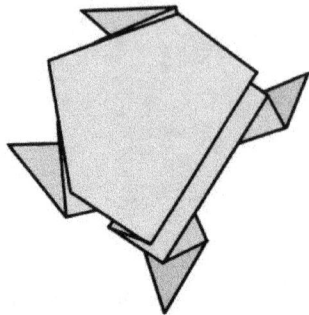 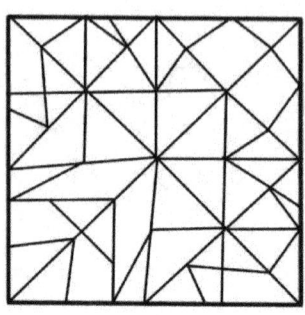

1 Beginne mit der weißen Seite nach oben.

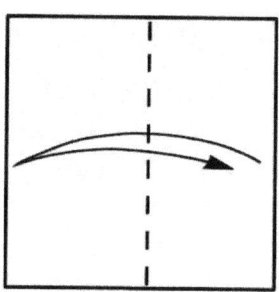

2 Falte und entfalten an gestrichelter Linie.

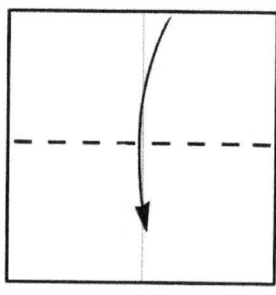

3 In der Hälfte falten.

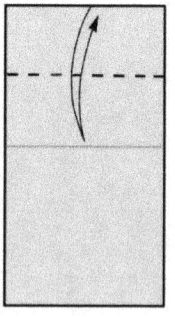

4 Zur Mitte falten und auffalten.

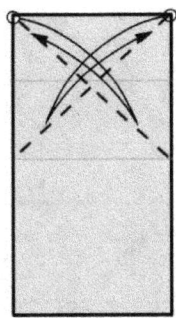 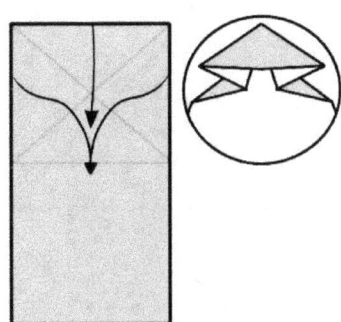

5 An der gestrichelten Linie falten und entfalten.

6 Taschenfaltung an den Falten.

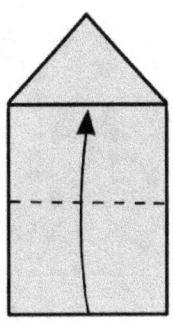 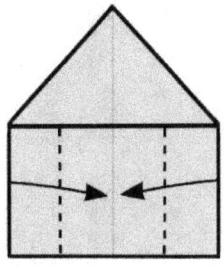

7 An der gestrichelten Linie nach oben falten.

8 Falte beide Seiten zur Mitte.

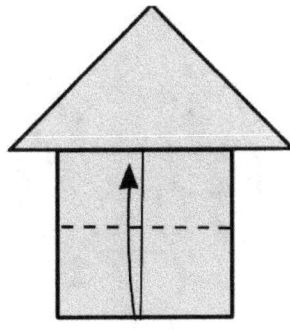 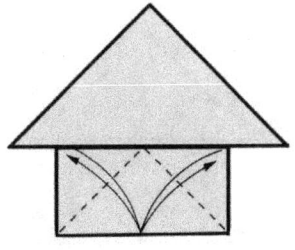

9 An gestrichelter Linie falten.

10 Falten und entfalten an gestrichelter Linie.

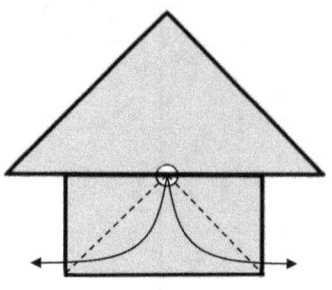 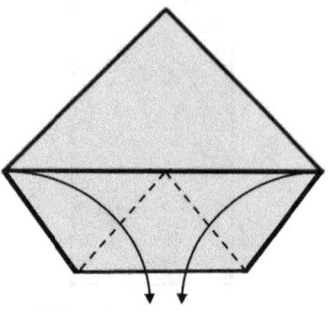

11 Taschen seitlich öffnen und glätten.

12 Falte die Lagen in der Mitte verbindend nach unten.

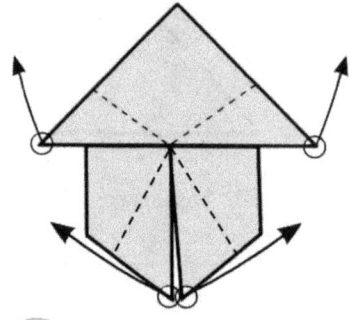 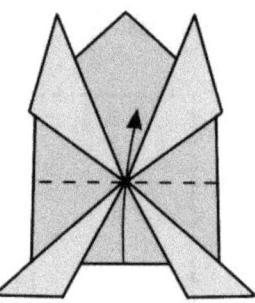

13 Falte nach oben um die Beine zu bilden.

14 Falte die gestrichelte Linie ein.

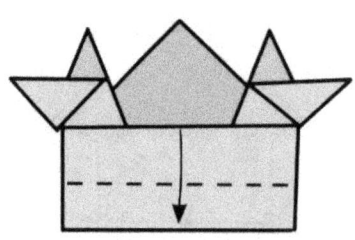 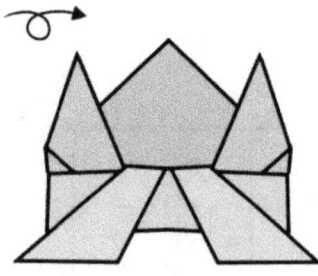

15 An der gestrichelten Linie auffalten.

16 Umdrehen.

17 Fertiger Frosch!

Schlange

 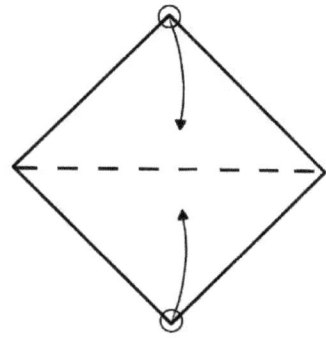

1 Beginne mit der weißen Seite nach oben.

2 Falte die Ecken zur Mitte.

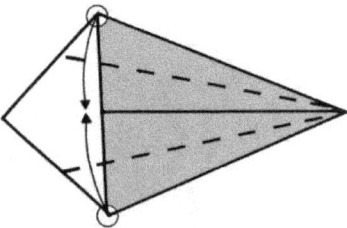 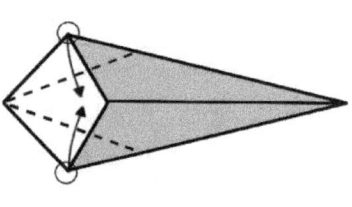

3 Falte die gestrichelten Linien ein.

4 Falte bis zum markierten Punkt.

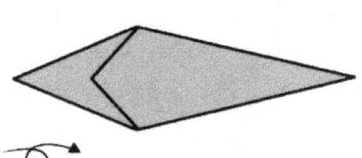
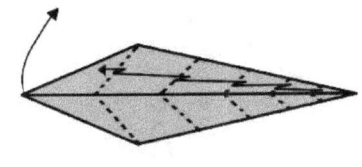

5 Drehe das Modell um.

6 Mach eine Stufenfaltung, indem du den linken Punkt nach oben faltest.

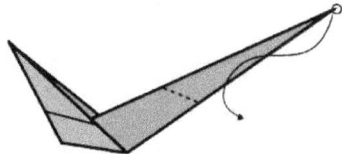
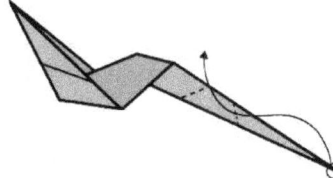

7 Falte die Tasche nach unten.

8 Falte die Tasche nach oben und unten, indem du Falten verwendest, um das Ende zu bilden.

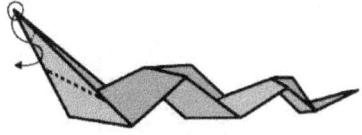

9 Falte den Kopf in die Tasche und falte die Spitze nach innen.

10 Fertige Schlange!

Blatt

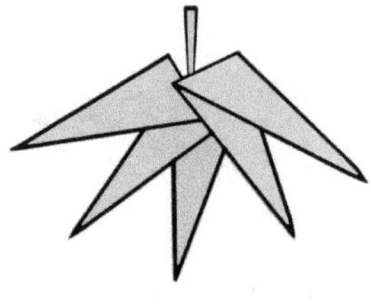
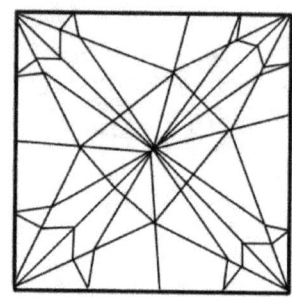

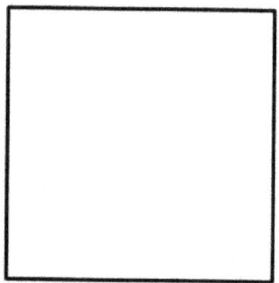
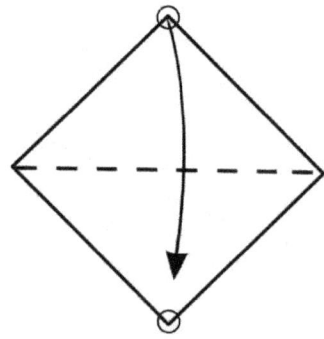

1. Beginne mit der weißen Seite nach oben.
2. Falte und entfalte in der Hälfte diagonal.

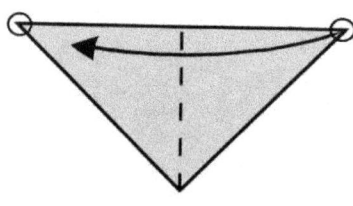
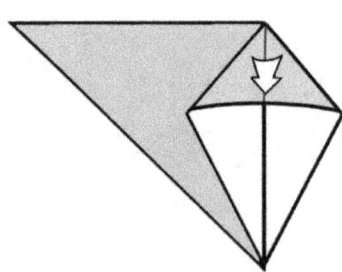

3. Falte das Modell an der markierten Stelle.
4. Quetschfalte die andere Seite.

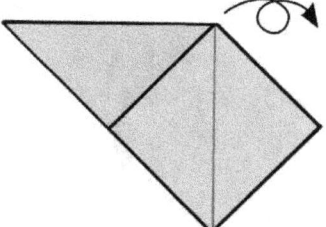
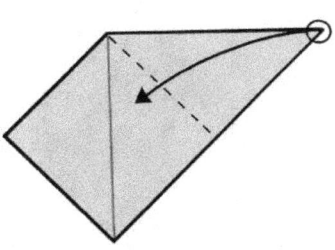

5 Drehe das Modell um.

6 Quetschfalte die andere Seite.

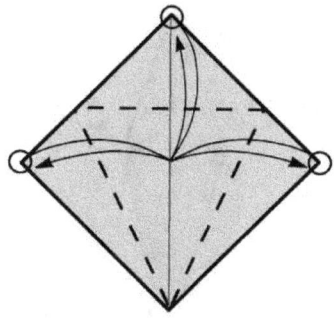
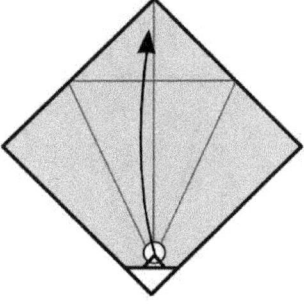

7 Falte und entfalte die linke, rechte und obere Ecke zur Mitte.

8 Hebe die untere Ecke nach oben.

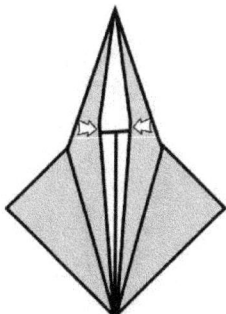
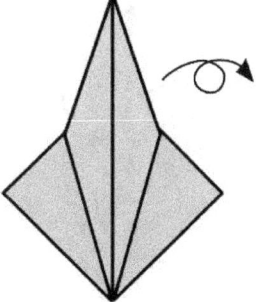

9 Falte die linke und rechte Seite zusammen.

10 Drehe das Modell um.

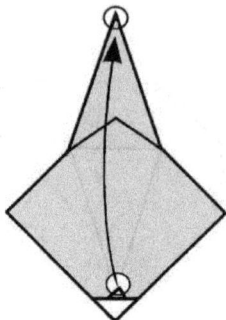
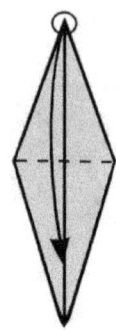

11 Hebe die untere Ecke an.

12 Falte die vordere Lage nach vorne und die hintere Lage nach hinten.

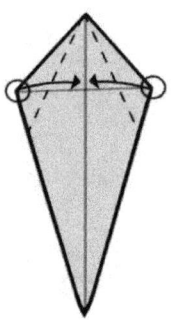
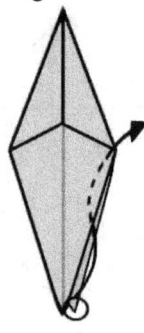

13 Falte die Ecken an die markierten Punkte.

14 Falte die hintere Lage an den markierten Punkt.

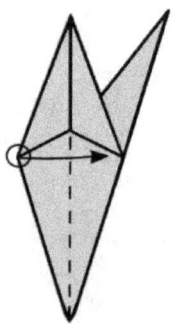
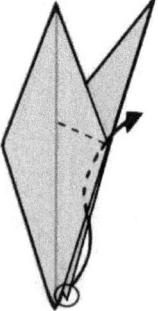

15 Falte die vordere linke Lage nach rechts.

16 Falte die hintere Lage in die Tasche.

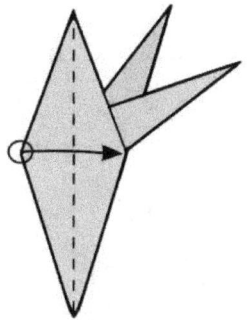 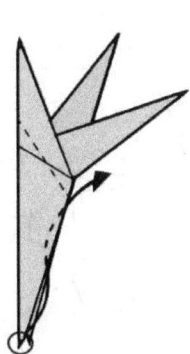

17 In der Hälfte falten.   **18** Falte die Taschenfalte an den gestrichelten Linien.

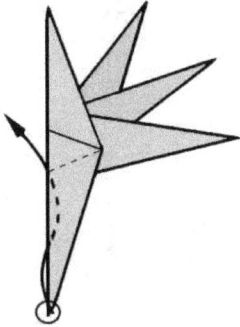 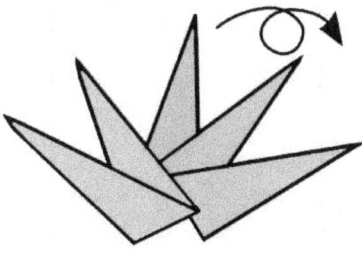

19 Falte bis zum markierten Punkt.   **20** Umdrehen.

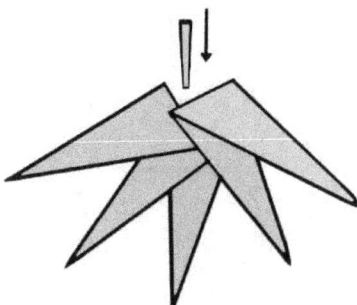 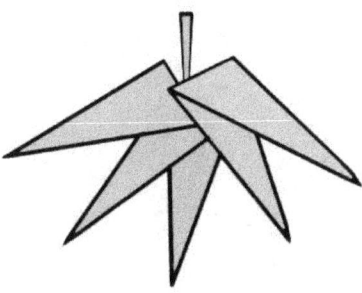

21 Einen Stiel hinzufügen.   **22** Fertiges Blatt!

Schwäne

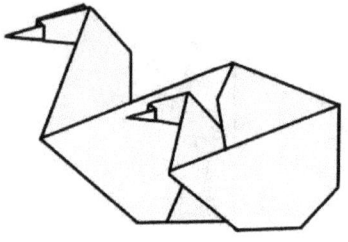 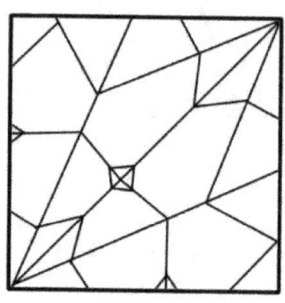

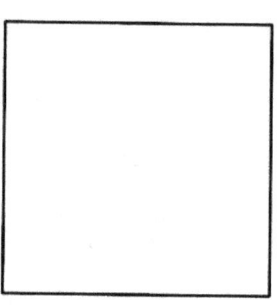

1. Beginne mit der weißen Seite nach oben.

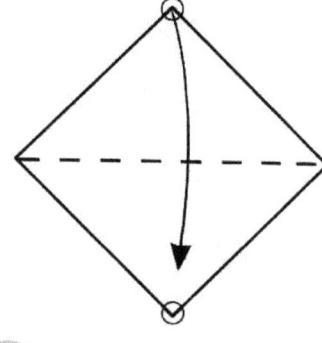

2. Falte und entfalte in der Hälfte diagonal.

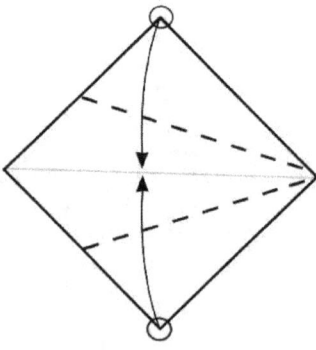

3. Falte das Modell an der markierten Stelle.

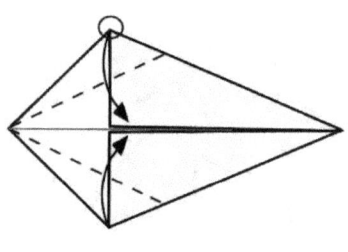

4. An den gestrichelten Linien zurückfalten.

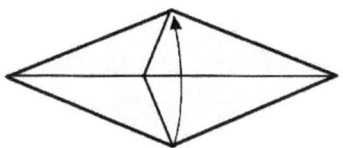 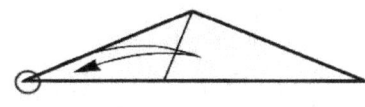

5 In der Hälfte falten. **6** An den gestrichelten Linien falten und auffalten.

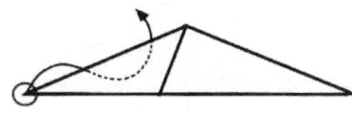 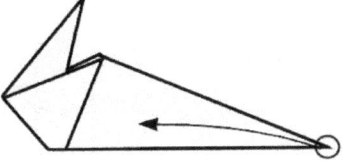

7 Taschenfalz an der gestrichelten Linie. **8** Markiertes Eck falten.

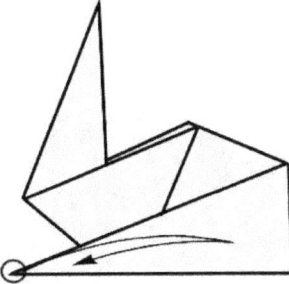 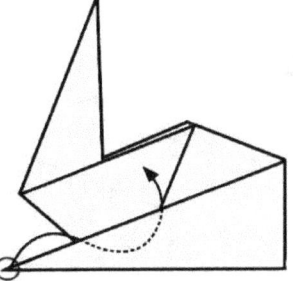

9 Zurückfalten und in der gestrichelten Linie auffalten. **10** Taschenfalte das Heck nach oben.

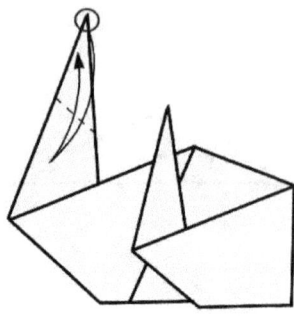 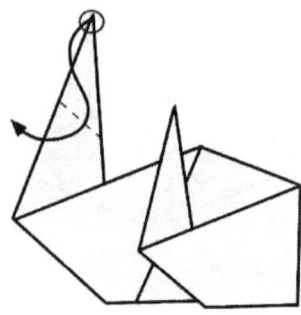

11 Falte, um eine Knickfalte zu bilden, und auffalten.   **12** Taschenfalte.

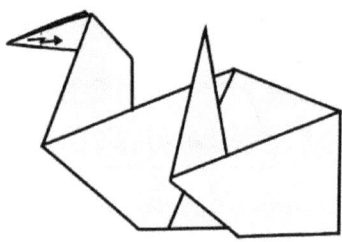 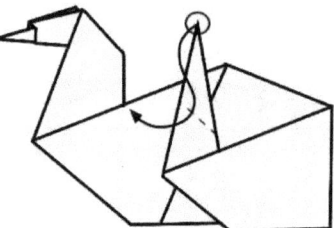

13 Schrittfalte zurück.   **14** Taschenfalte in der gestrichelten Linie.

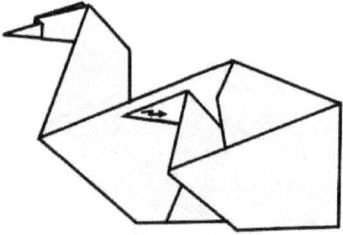 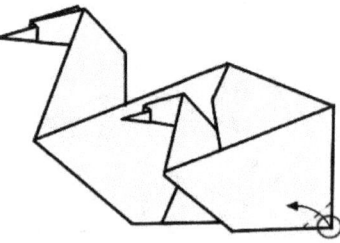

15 Schrittfalte für Schnabel.   **16** Taschenfalte nach innen.

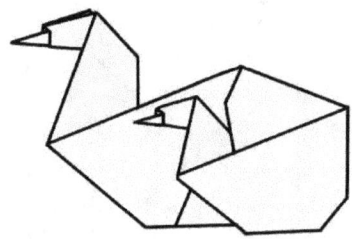

17 Fertige Schwäne!

Garnele

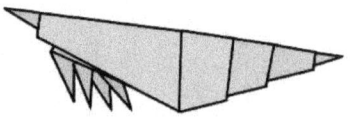
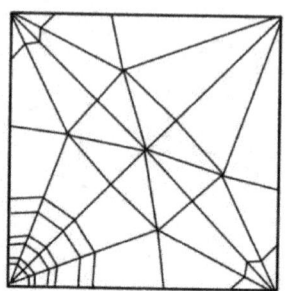

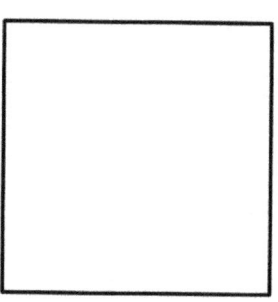

1. Beginne mit der weißen Seite nach oben.

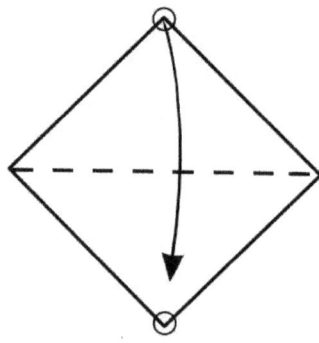

2. Falte und entfalte in der Hälfte diagonal.

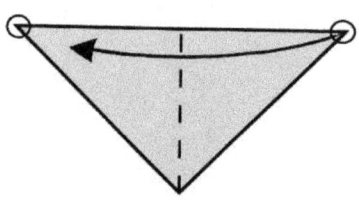

3. Falte das Modell an der markierten Stelle.

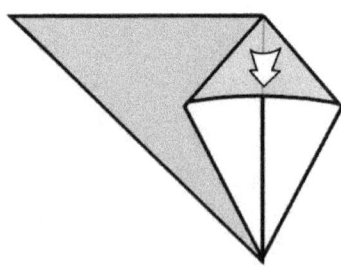

4. Quetschfalte die vordere Lage.

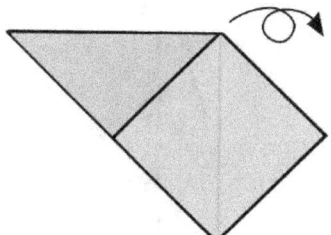
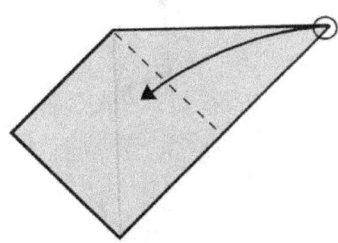

5 Drehe das Modell um.

6 Quetschfalte die andere Seite.

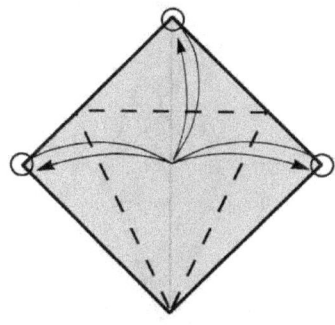
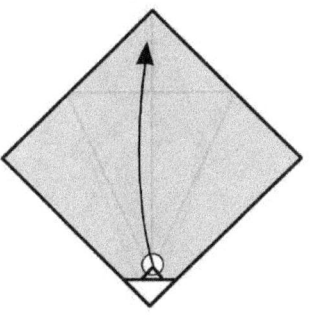

7 Falte und entfalte die linke, rechte und obere Ecke zur Mitte.

8 Hebe die untere Ecke nach oben.

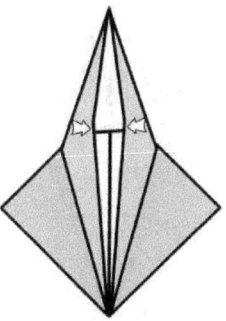
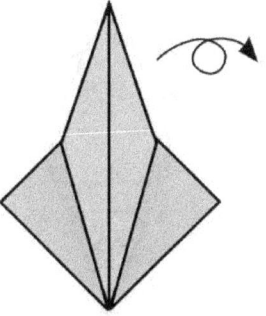

9 Quetschfalte die linke und rechte Seite.

10 Drehe das Modell um.

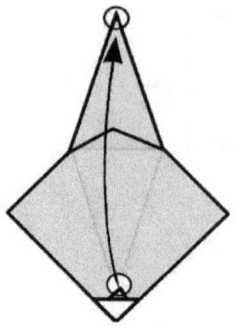
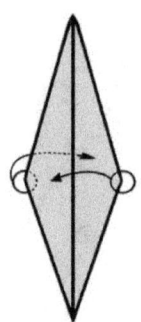

11 Hebe die untere Ecke an.

12 Falte die rechte vordere Lage nach links und die linke hintere Lage nach rechts.

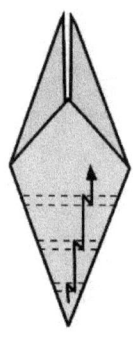
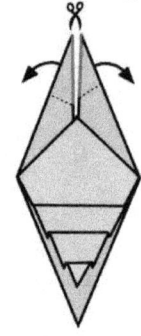

13 Falte die vordere Lage schrittweise.

14 Schneide und falte Lagen nach hinten.

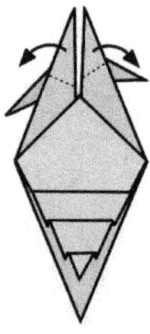
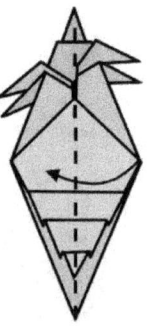

15 Vordere Lage nach hinten falten.

16 In der Hälfte falten.

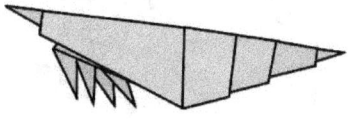

17 Fertige Garnele!

Affe

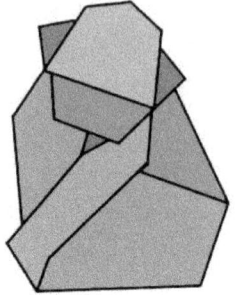 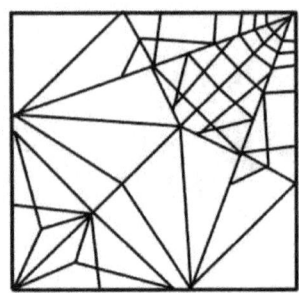

 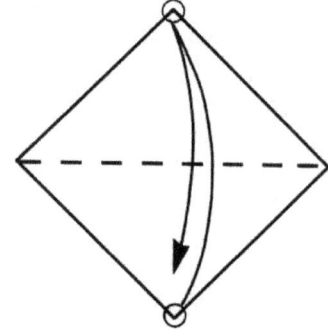

1 Beginne mit der weißen Seite nach oben.

2 Falte und entfalte in der Hälfte diagonal.

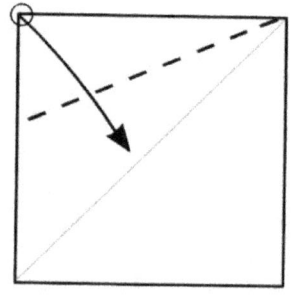 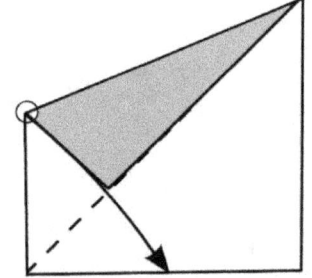

3 Falte zur Mitte.

4 An der gestrichelten Linie falten.

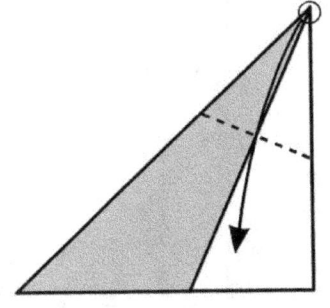 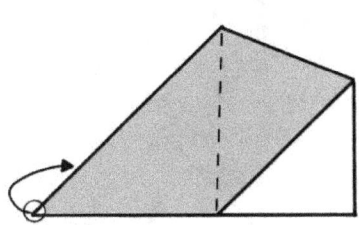

5 An der gestrichelten Linie nach unten falten.

6 Zurückfalten.

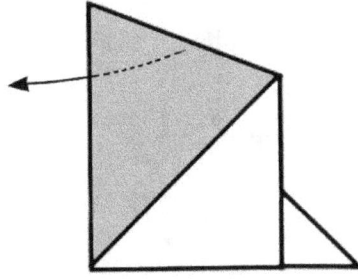 

7 Ziehe die Innentasche heraus.

8 An der gestrichelten Linie falten und auffalten.

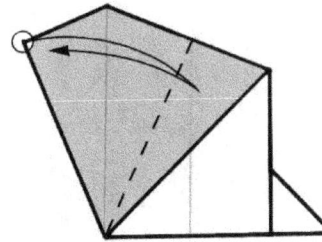 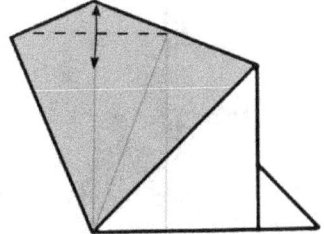

9 An der gestrichelten Linie falten und auffalten.

10 Falte und entfalte den oberen Punkt.

47

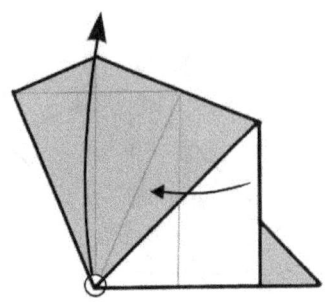

11 Falte die rechte Seite nach innen.

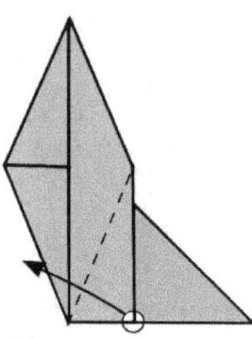

12 Diagonal nach oben falten.

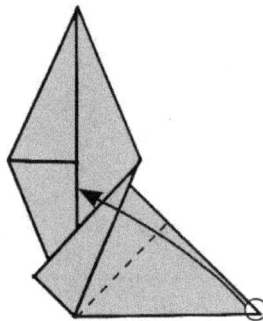

13 Falte die gestrichelte Linie ein.

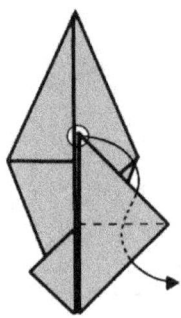

14 Mach eine Taschenfaltung.

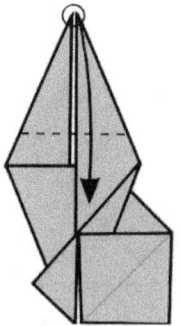

15 Falte an der gestrichelten Linie nach unten.

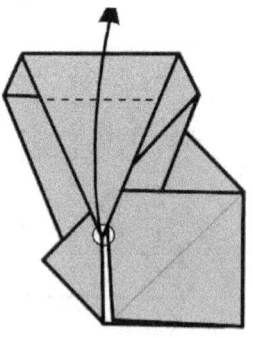

16 Falte nach oben.

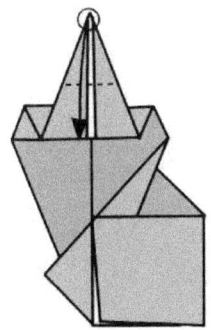
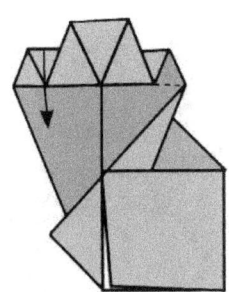

17 An der gestrichelten Linie nach unten falten.

18 Falte die Lagen nach unten.

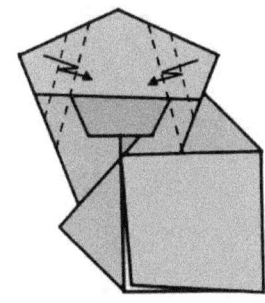
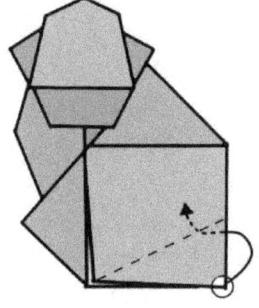

19 Mach eine Stufenfaltung nach innen.

20 Mach eine Taschenfalte nach innen.

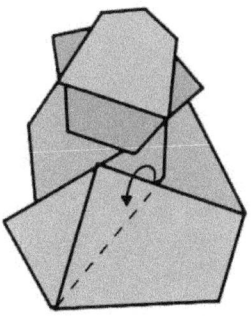
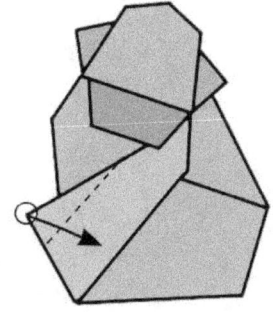

21 Ziehe die hintere Ebene heraus.

22 Nach innen falten.

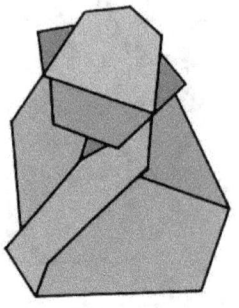

23 Fertiger Affe!

Ente

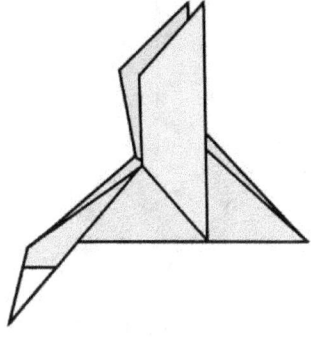 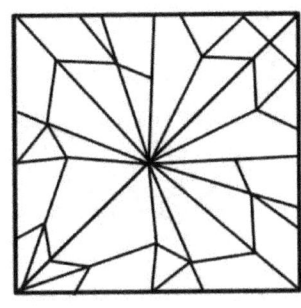

 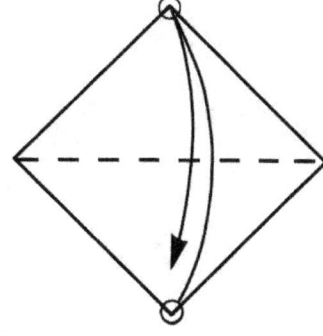

1. Beginne mit der weißen Seite nach oben.

2. Falte und entfalte in der Hälfte diagonal.

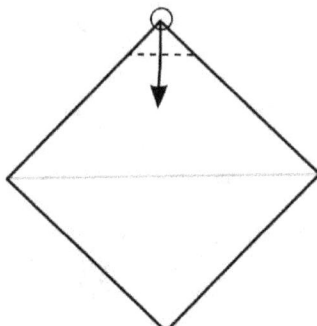 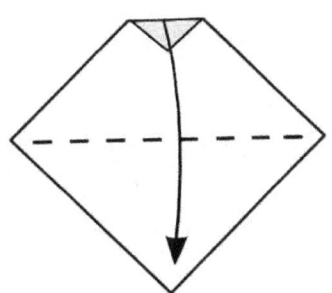

3. Falte die Spitze nach unten.

4. In der Hälfte diagonal falten.

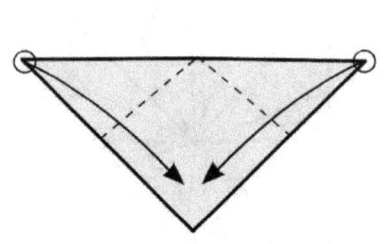
5 Falte die beiden Seiten diagonal nach unten.

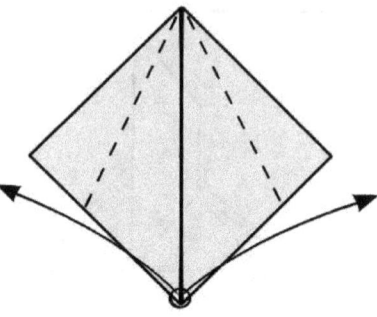
6 An den gestrichelten Linien auffalten.

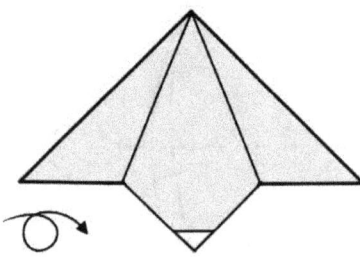
7 Drehe das Modell um.

8 Falte die beiden Seiten zur Mitte.

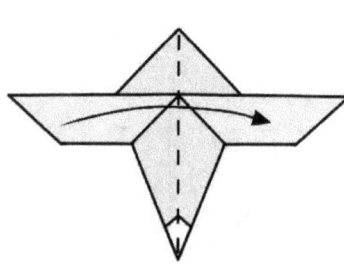
9 In der Hälfte falten.

10 Drehe das Modell.

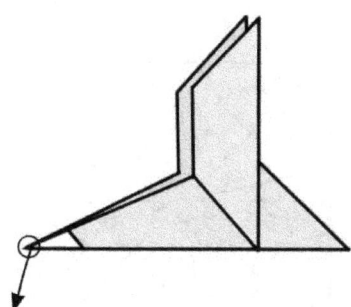
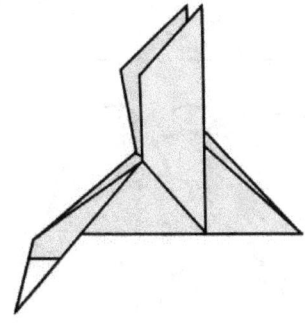

11 Taschenfalte nach unten, um den Kopf zu bilden.

12 Fertige Ente!

Lilie

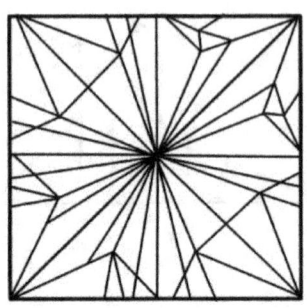

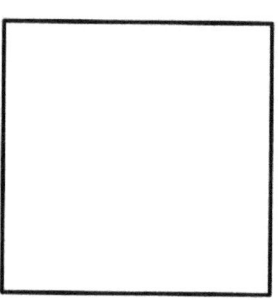
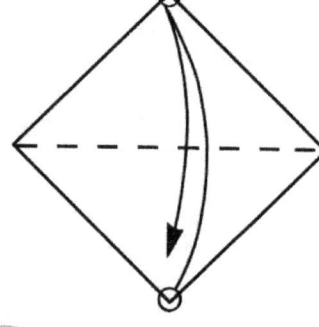

1. Beginne mit der weißen Seite nach oben.
2. Falte und entfalte in der Hälfte diagonal.

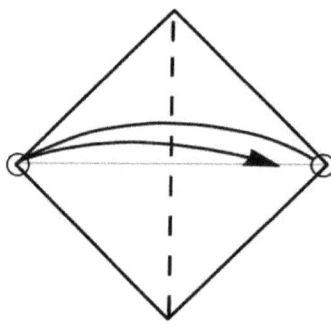
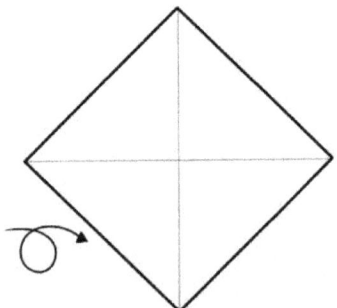

3. Falte und entfalte in der anderen Diagonale.
4. Drehe das Modell um.

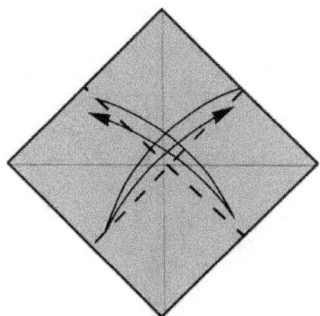

5 Falte und entfalte an der gestrichelten Linie.

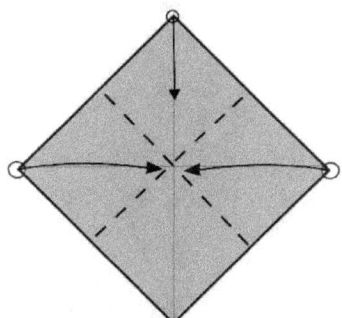

6 Mach eine Taschenfaltung mit den im vorherigen Schritt erstellen Falten.

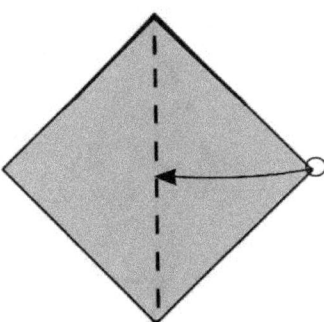

7 Öffne die rechte Ecke.

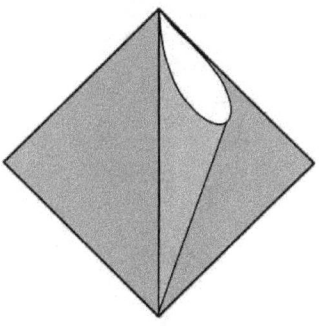

8 Mach eine Quetschfalte.

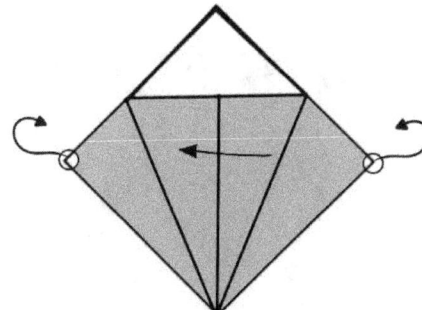

9 Wiederhole Schritte 7 und 8 für die anderen Seiten.

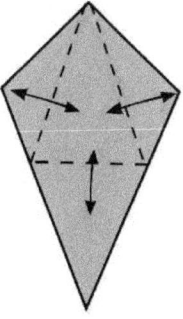

10 Falte und entfalte an den gestrichelten Linien.

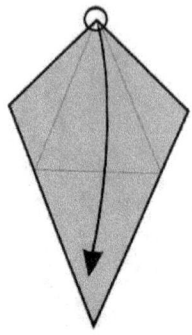

11 Falte an den Falten nach unten.

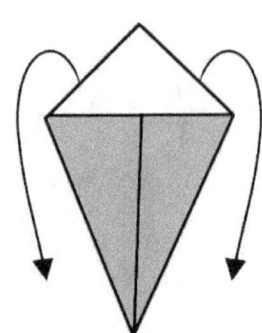

12 Wiederhole den Vorgang für die anderen Seiten.

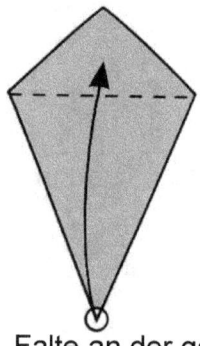

13 Falte an der gestrichelten Linie nach oben.

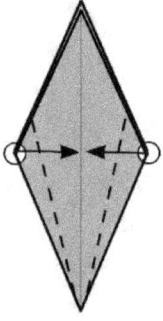

14 Falte zur Mitte.

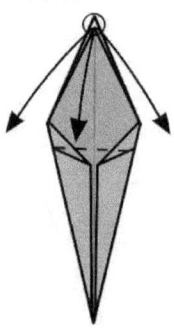

15 Falte an den gestrichelten Linien nach unten.

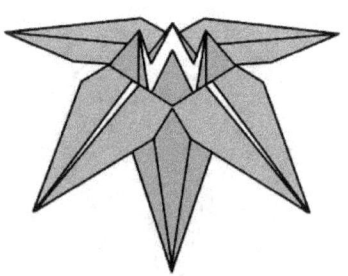

16 Fertige Lilie!

Pinguin

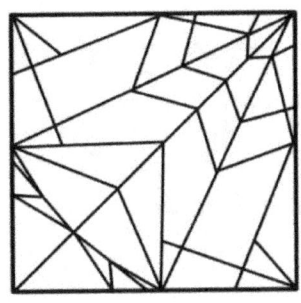

1. Beginne mit der weißen Seite nach oben.

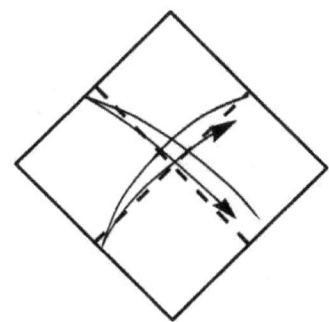
2. Falte und entfalte an den gestrichelten Linien.

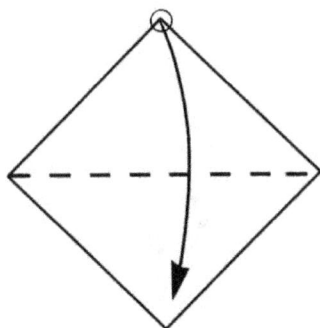
3. In der Hälfte falten.

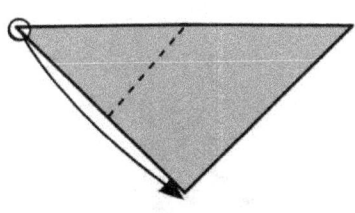
4. Mach eine Taschenfaltung bis zum markierten Punkt.

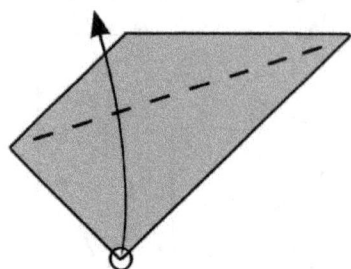
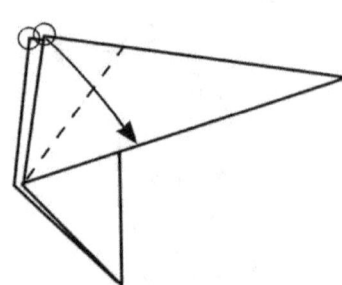

5 Falte die beiden Seiten nach oben.

6 Falte an den gestrichelten Linien nach unten.

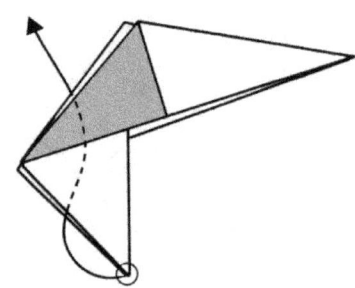
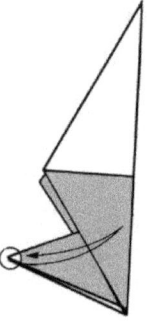

7 Mach eine Taschenfalte und drehe das Modell.

8 Falte und entfalte bis zum markierten Punkt.

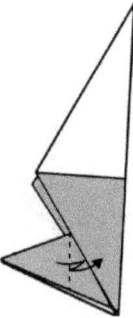
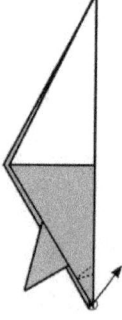

9 Mach eine Stufenfaltung.

10 Diagonal nach oben falten, um die Beine zu bilden.

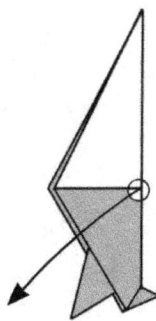
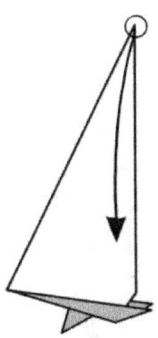

11 Öffne die Falte. **12** Falte nach unten.

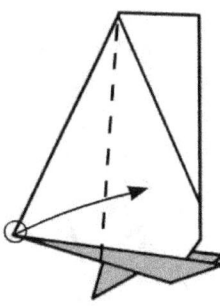
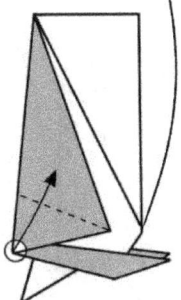

13 Falte die gestrichelten Linien ein, um Flügel zu bilden. **14** Falte die in Schritt 12 gefaltete Lage nach innen und entfalte sie.

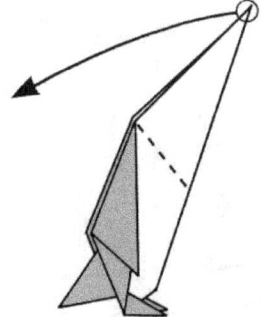
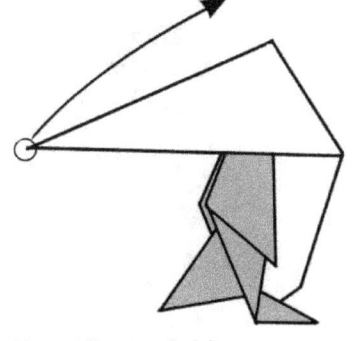

15 Falte an der gestrichelten Linie diagonal nach unten. **16** Entfalten.

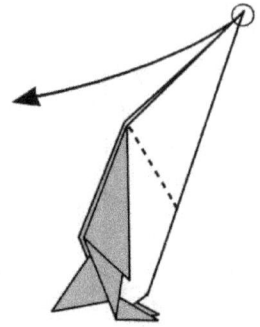 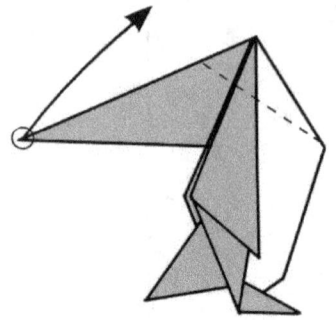

17 Diagonal nach unten falten.

18 An der gestrichelten Linie falten.

19 Falte bis zum markierten Punkt.

20 Taschenfalte, um den Kopf zu bilden.

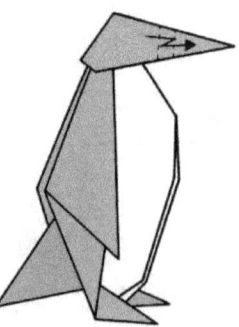 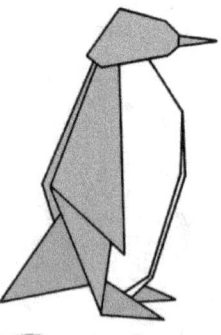

21 Mach eine Stufenfaltung.

22 Fertiger Pinguin!

Gürteltier

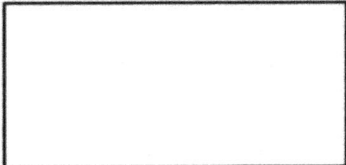
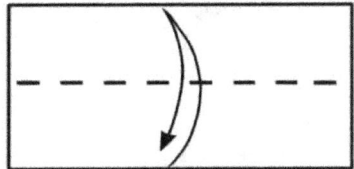

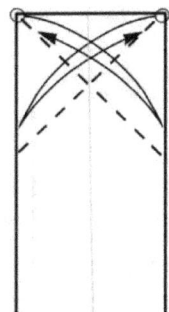
1 Beginne mit der weißen Seite nach oben.

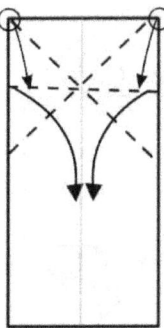
2 In der Hälfte falten und entfalten.

3 Falte und entfalte an den gestrichelten Linien.

4 Mach eine Taschenfaltung an den gestrichelten Linien.

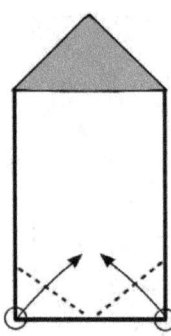 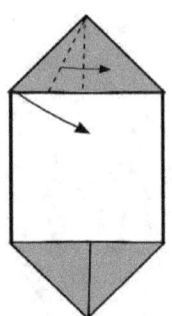

5 Falte die Ecken diagonal nach oben.

6 Falte die linke Ecke zur Mitte; mach eine Taschenfalte an gestrichelter Linie.

7 Falte mit einer Taschenfalte nach oben.

8 Falte die Spitze nach unten.

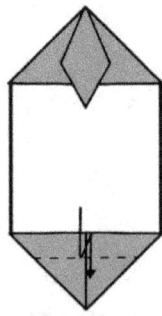 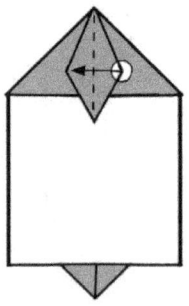

9 Mach eine Rückwärtsfalte an der gestrichelten Linie.

10 Falte die rechte Ecke nach links.

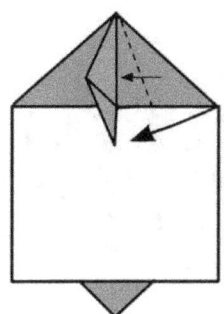
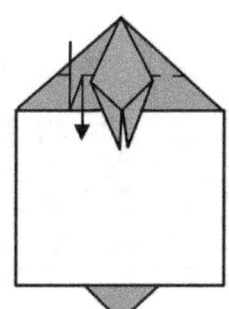

11 Wie in Schritt 6 die andere Seite falten.

12 Falte die hintere Lage schrittweise nach unten.

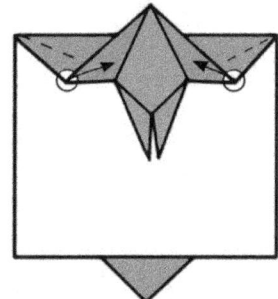
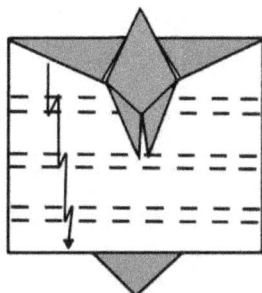

13 Falte an den gestrichelten Linien zurück.

14 Mach eine Stufenfaltung.

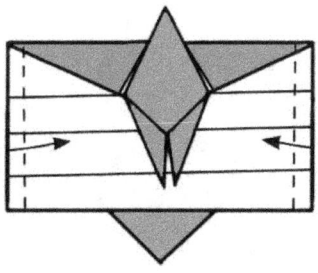
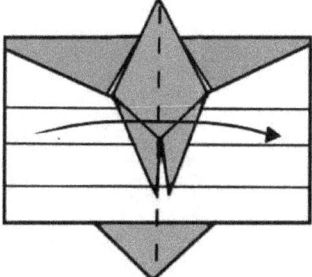

15 Falte die Ecken nach innen.

16 Falte in der Hälfte.

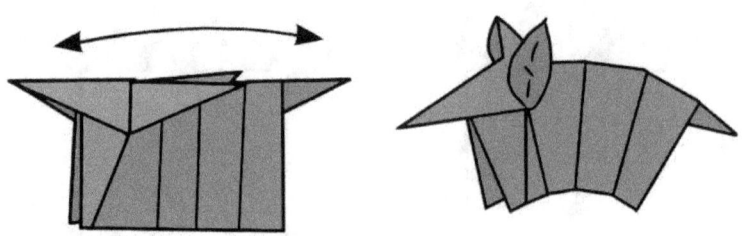

17 Mach den Körper runder und öffne die Ohren.

18 Fertiges Gürteltier!

Krebs

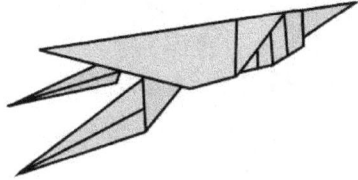
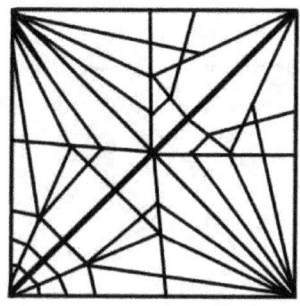

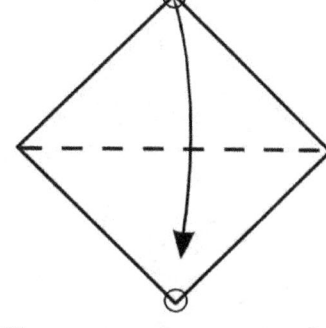

1. Beginne mit der weißen Seite nach oben.
2. Falte und entfalte in der Hälfte diagonal.

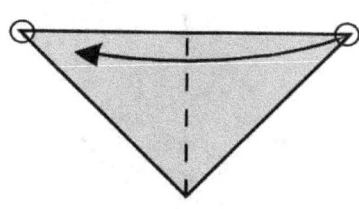
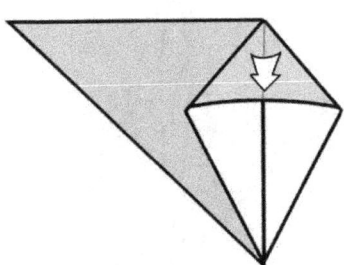

3. Falte das Modell an der markierten Stelle.
4. Quetschfalte die vordere Lage.

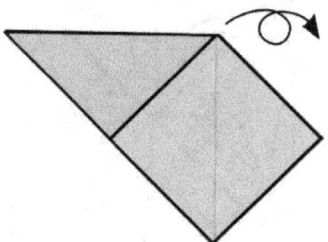
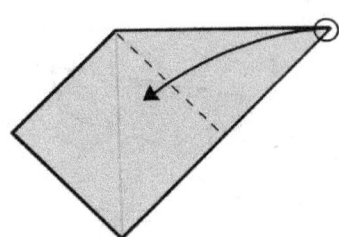

5 Drehe das Modell um.

6 Quetschfalte die andere Seite.

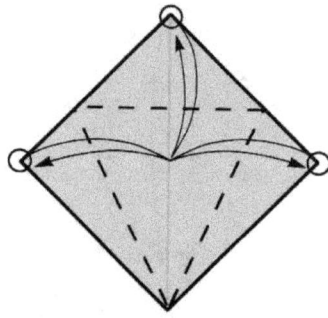
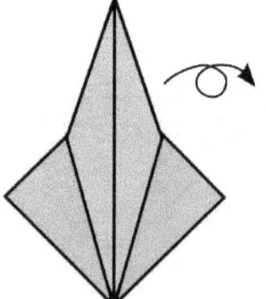

7 Falte und entfalte die linken, rechten und oberen Ecken zur Mitte.

8 Hebe die untere Ecke nach oben.

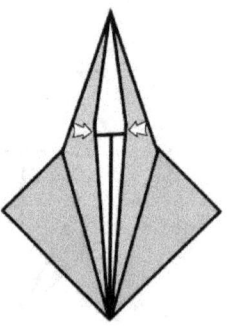

9 Falte die linke und rechte Seite zusammen.

10 Drehe das Modell um.

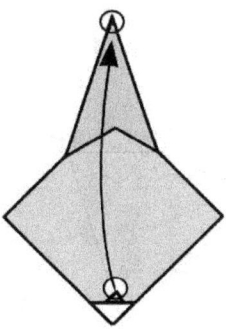
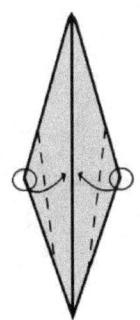

11 Hebe die untere Ecke an.

12 Falte die Ecken zur Mitte.

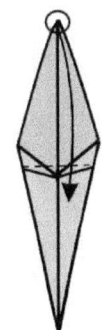
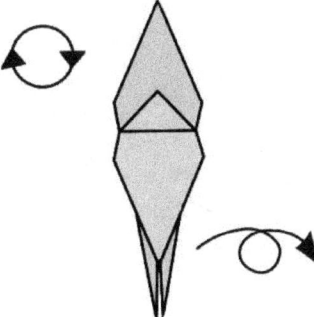

13 Falte die gestrichelte Linie ein.

14 Drehe und wende das Modell.

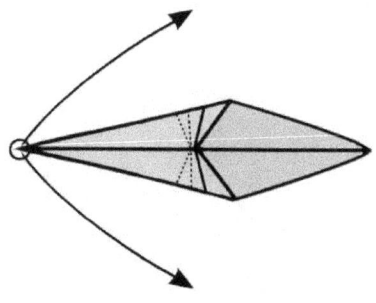
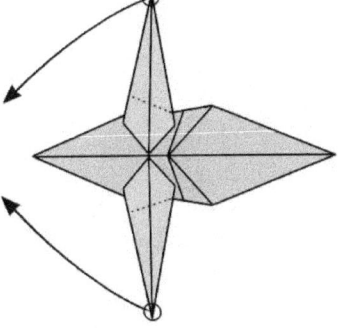

15 Beide Seiten nach rechts falten und flachdrücken.

16 Falte die gestrichelten Linien ein.

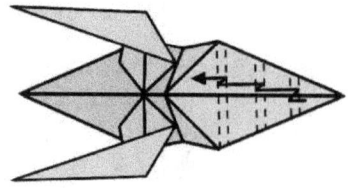 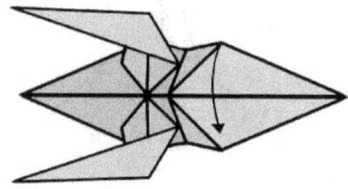

17 Falte die vorderen Lagen an den gestrichelten Linien.

18 Falte in der Hälfte.

19 Fertiger Krebs!

Schnecke

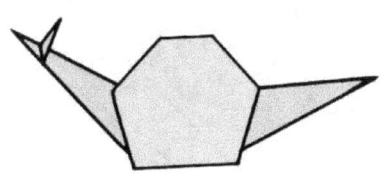
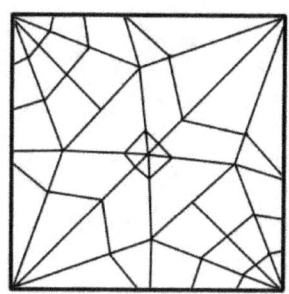

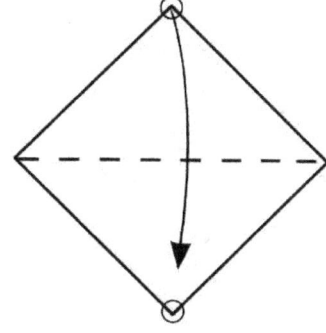

1. Beginne mit der weißen Seite nach oben.
2. Falte und entfalte in der Hälfte diagonal.

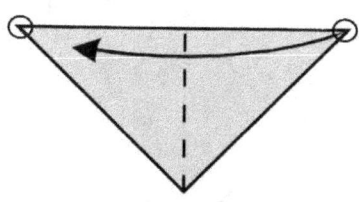
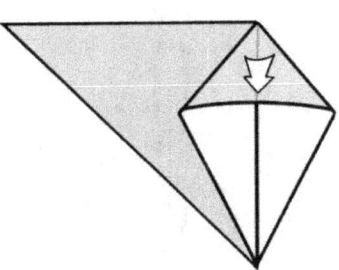

3. Falte das Modell an der markierten Stelle.
4. Quetschfalte die vordere Lage.

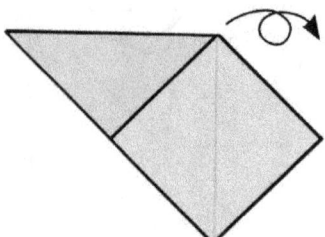
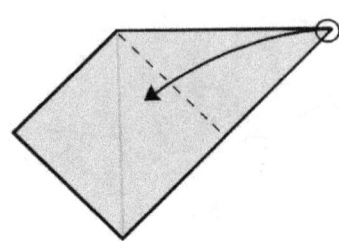

5 Drehe das Modell um.

6 Quetschfalte die andere Seite.

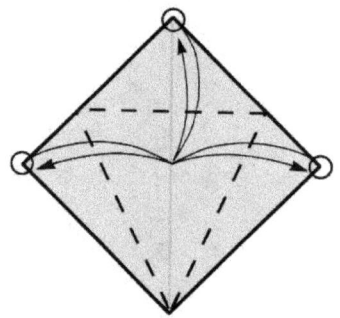
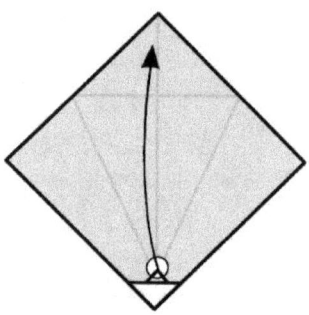

7 Falte und entfalte die linken, rechten und oberen Ecken zur Mitte.

8 Hebe die untere Ecke nach oben.

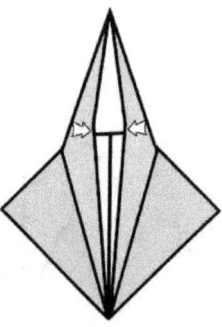
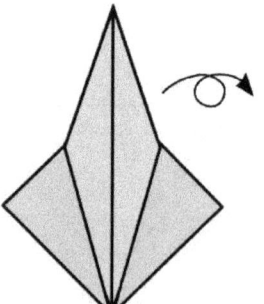

9 Falte die linke und rechte Seite zusammen.

10 Drehe das Modell um.

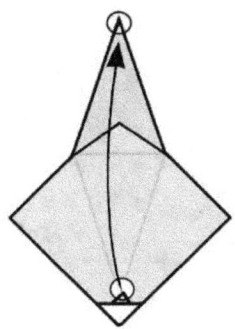
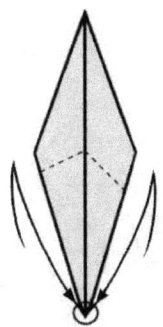

11 Hebe die untere Ecke an.

12 Klappe die Ecken nach oben und entfalte sie.

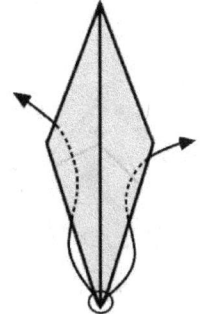
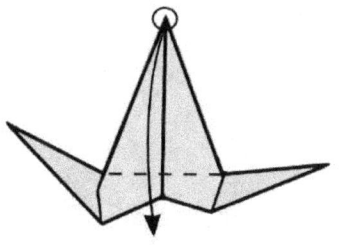

13 Falte die linke und rechte Ecke in die Tasche.

14 Falte an den gestrichelten Linien nach unten.

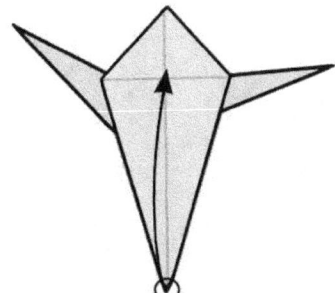
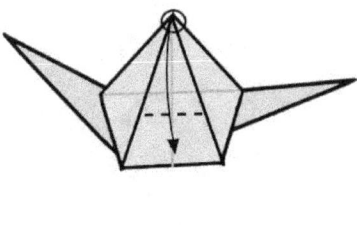

15 Falte an den gestrichelten Linien nach oben.

16 Falte an den gestrichelten Linien nach unten.

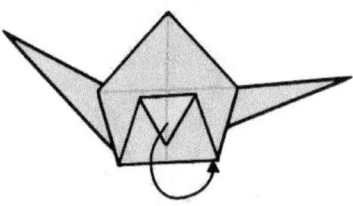 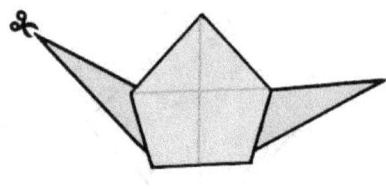

17 Falte die Lagen nach hinten.

18 Schneide und trenne die Lagen.

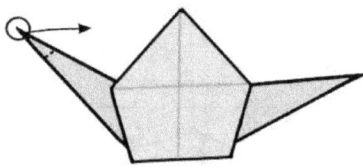 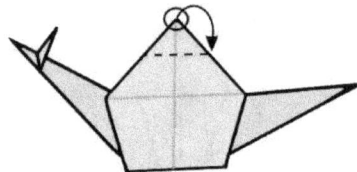

19 Falte die vordere Lage zurück.

20 Falte die Spitze zurück.

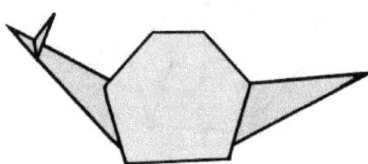

21 Fertige Schnecke!

Krokodil

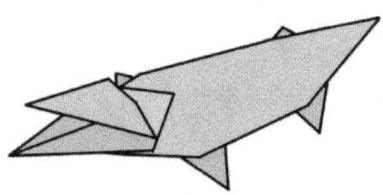
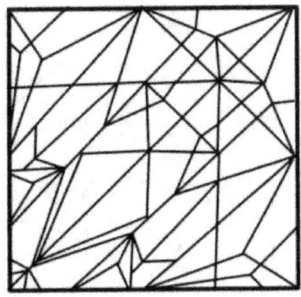

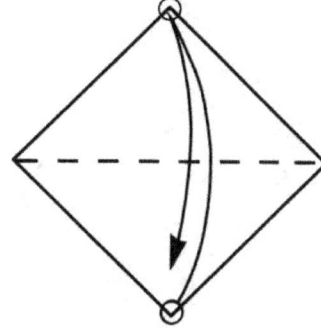

1. Beginne mit der weißen Seite nach oben.
2. Falte und entfalte in der Hälfte diagonal.

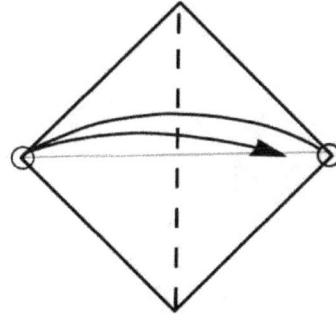
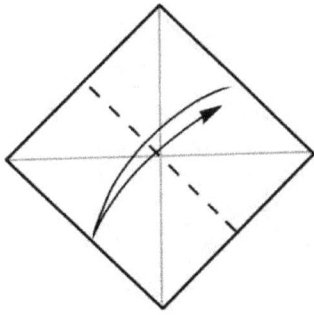

3. Falte und entfalte in der anderen Hälfte diagonal.
4. In der Hälfte falten und entfalten.

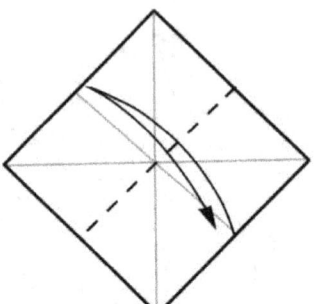

5 In der Hälfte falten und auffalten.

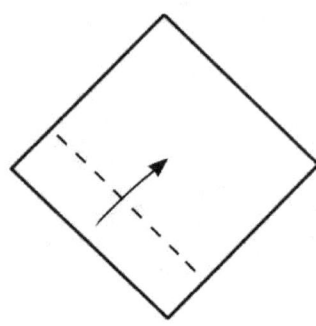

6 An der gestrichelten Linie falten.

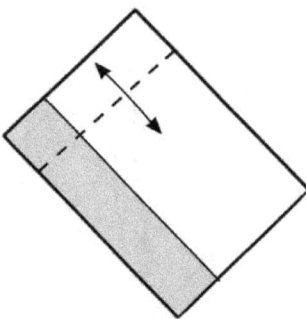

7 An der gestrichelten Linie falten und auffalten.

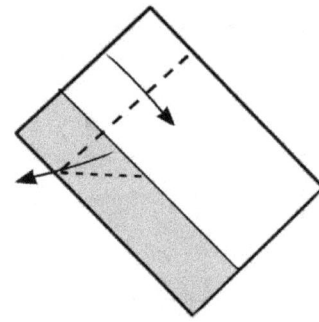

8 An der gestrichelten Linie nach unten falten und die Kante nach außen ziehen.

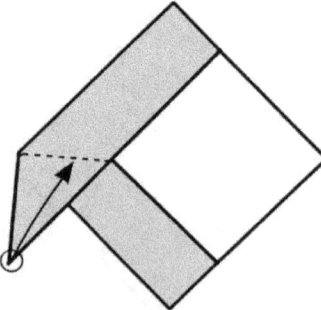

9 Mach eine Taschenfaltung.

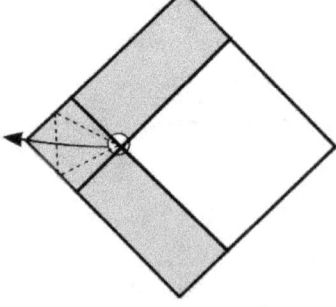

10 Falte die Taschenfalte an den gestrichelten Linien.

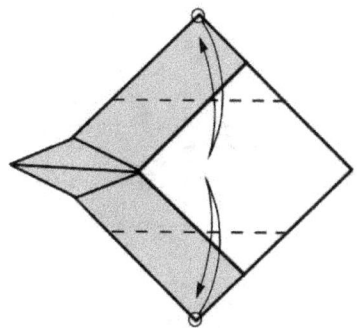 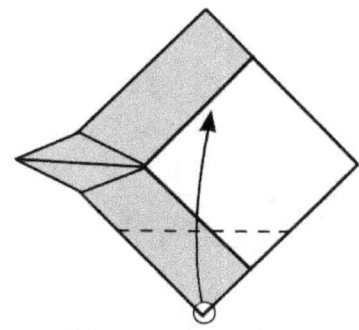

11 Falte und entfalte an den gestrichelten Linien.

12 Nach oben falten.

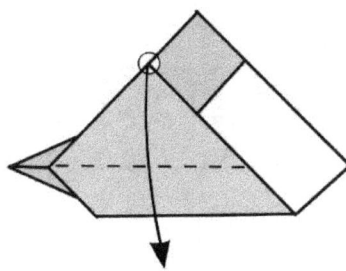 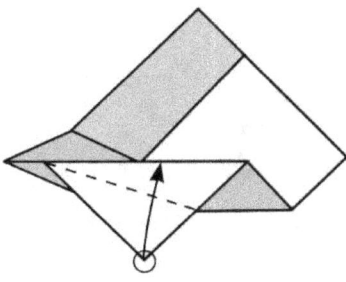

13 An der gestrichelten Linie auffalten.

14 An der gestrichelten Linie nach oben falten.

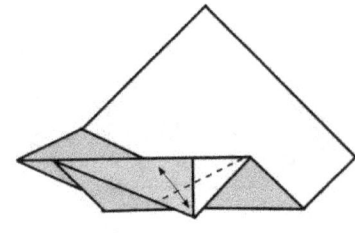 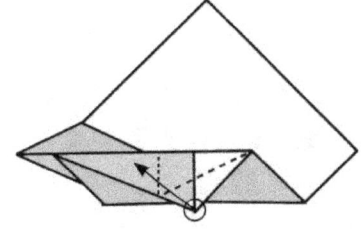

15 An der gestrichelten Linie falten und entfalten.

16 Mach eine Taschenfaltung an den Falten.

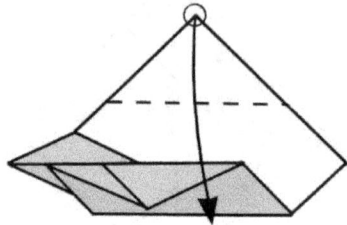
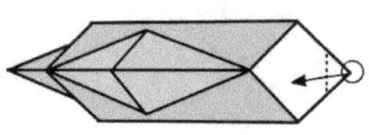

17 Wiederhole die vorherigen Schritte für die andere Seite.

18 Falte den Punkt an der gestrichelten Linie.

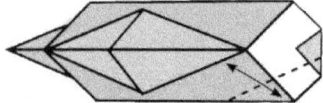
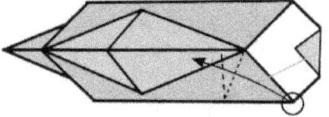

19 Falte und entfalte an der gestrichelten Linie.

20 Mach eine Taschenfaltung.

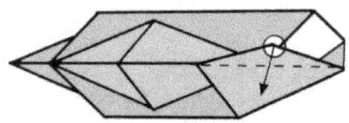
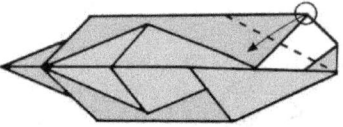

21 Nach innen falten.

22 Mach dasselbe mit der anderen Seite.

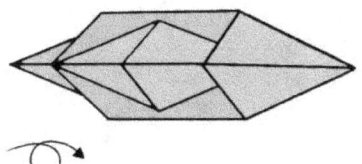
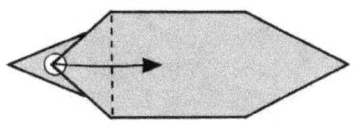

23 Dreh das Modell um. 24 Falte nach rechts.

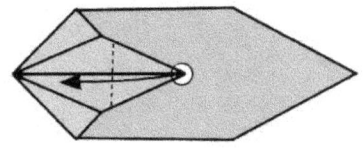
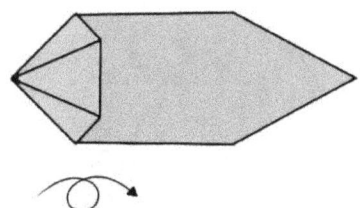

25 Falte die gestrichelte Linie ein. 26 Umdrehen.

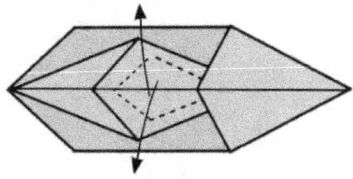
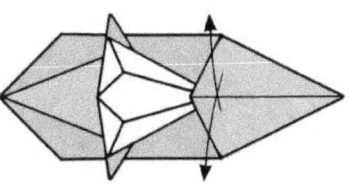

27 Öffne die Taschen. 28 Öffne die Taschen.

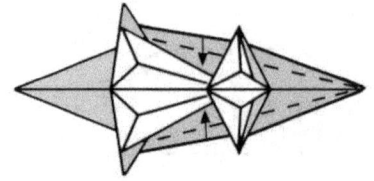
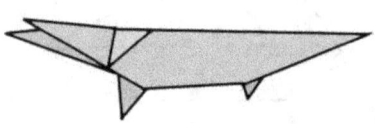

29 Falte die Innenseite an den gestrichelten Linien.

30 Fertiges Krokodil!

Vogel

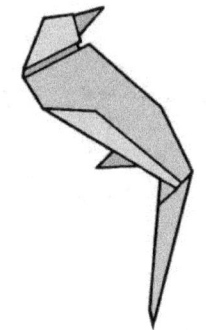 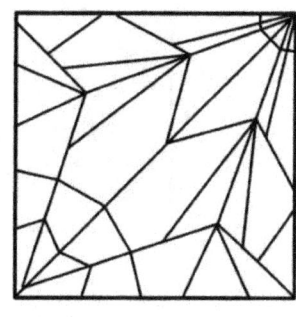

1 Beginne mit der weißen Seite nach oben.

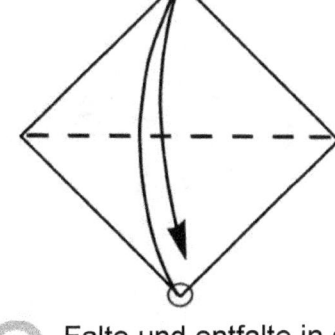

2 Falte und entfalte in der Hälfte diagonal.

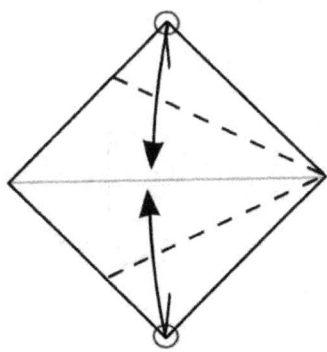

3 Falte die Ecken zur Mitte und entfalte sie.

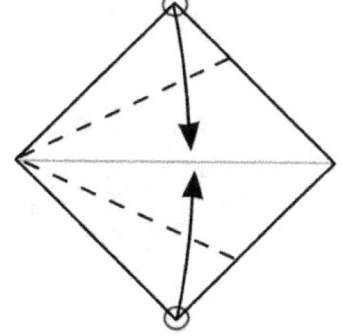

4 An den gestrichelten Linien falten.

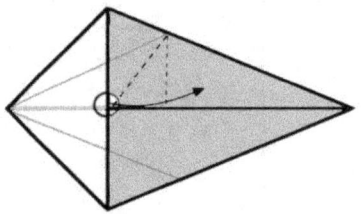
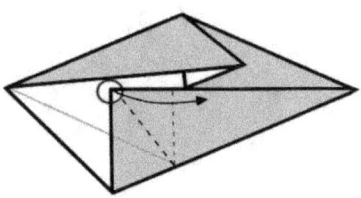

5 Falte die gestrichelte Linie ein, um eine Tasche zu bilden.

6 Falte die andere Seite.

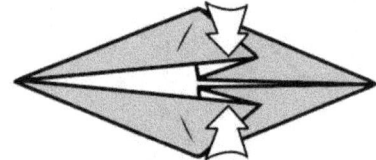
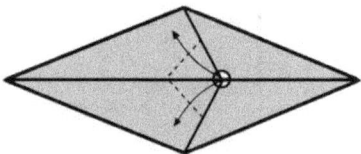

7 Glätte die Taschen.

8 Falte die beiden Seiten an den gestrichelten Linien.

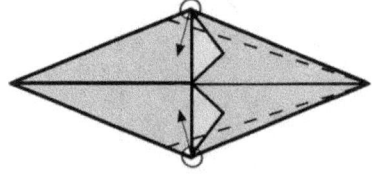
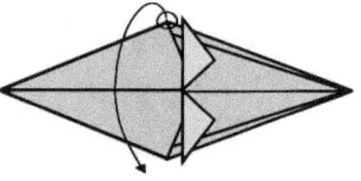

9 Falte die beiden Seiten an den gestrichelten Linien.

10 In der Hälfte falten.

11 Taschenfalte, um den Schwanz zu bilden.

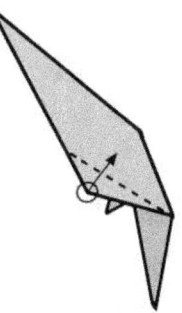

12 Falte die beiden Seiten an den gestrichelten Linien nach innen.

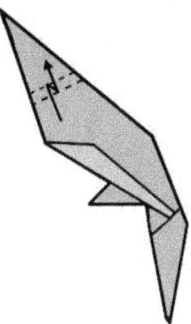

13 Mach einen Stufenfalz.

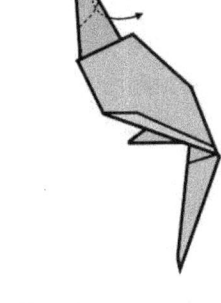

14 Falte den Kopf in die Tasche.

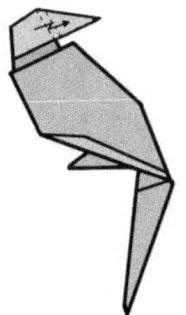

15 Mach eine Stufenfaltung und falte die Spitze nach unten, um einen Schnabel zu bilden.

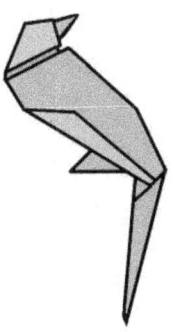

16 Fertiger Vogel!

P.S. Darf ich um einen Gefallen bitten?

Zunächst einmal vielen Dank, dass Sie dieses Buch **Origami Buch für Beginner 3** erworben haben. Ich weiß, dass Sie sich eine beliebige Anzahl von Büchern hätten aussuchen können, aber Sie haben sich für dieses Buch entschieden, und dafür bin ich Ihnen sehr dankbar.

Wenn Ihnen dieses Buch gefallen hat und Sie es als nützlich empfunden haben, würde ich mich freuen von Ihnen zu hören und hoffe, dass Sie sich etwas Zeit zum Schreiben einer Rezension nehmen können wenn möglich.

Ihr Feedback und Ihre Unterstützung werden dem Autor helfen, zukünftige Projekte zu verbessern und dieses Buch noch besser zu machen.

DANKE!
=)

How I Learnt About Concrete

It was the winter of my brother's breakdown
when the police, a squad of social workers took him.
My dad exiled himself in the backyard
to build pathways, walls, a greenhouse base.

His hands dissolved in dust,
fingernails softened in martyrdom,
body, heart of his own machine.

He covered all greenery in flatness, logic,
angles of the geometric dream of his unmixed being.

What I learnt then; I still use. I know the perfect mix:
how much powder, water, sand to pad, strengthen,
the correct percentages, ideal textures.

I will always see it, the fire of his tiny lamps
in the darkened garden on those December evenings
that allowed him to work into the night, merge with it,
whilst his wife, my sister and I watched;
set ourselves firmly in the kitchen window;
wished him to finish, come back to us
from wherever he had been.

Where He Lived

For fifty years we played chess.
He always won.

We played: through my brother's madness,
his mother's death,
our four times moving houses,
Watergate,
the fall of the Berlin Wall, 9-11.

He played on winter evenings
with his colleagues from his work,
those discreet men who visited in tidy jackets,
tweed or thick deep blue
pressed cotton and shined shoes,
who sat silent in our sour lamp light.

There was never conversation.
This was beyond words;
where my father and his friends
would meet on inner landscapes
and made walls, bridges with each move.

Talking was for the dumb.

When he was dying, I let him win.

Not that I ever broke through
and saw those fields, meadows,
the cities he had built from strategies,
plots in rarefied air;
or witnessed his higher architecture,
calculations,
buildings where he lived
hidden higher up;
two, three moves ahead.

Wearing the Dead

I wear their pyjamas. That way I bring them back,
keep them with me, have company
without the embarrassment, inconvenience,
of having to talk to them; explain to my wife
why somebody she cannot see is whispering to me.

It started with my dad's pjs, barely worn.

A few pairs with tears, undefinable stains.
One stain, if you looked at it sideways,
appeared to be a map of Scotland.

Then it was thrift store buys.
Plaids, concentric patterns,
designs of previous decades, saggy elastic,
an apocalypse of broken knees.

People live on through me.
Sure, some may have families to remember them
yet this is fair, anonymous, equal,
with no judgement.

This is me now. A life in solid, dependable nightwear.
Warm, reliable in eternal winters
that can be worn in the family home
with no embarrassment, no inconvenience caused.

The dead can be surprisingly considerate.
Often, they bring them themselves;
form orderly queues on the lawn.

Look, there is my dad with his new family
holding out their neat little cotton bundles:
ironed, warmed, with a tinge of sulphur,
ready to wear.

My Inheritance

My children. How I love them.
How I want them to go away.

I'm a man.
I should manage money,
command a department,
balance on girders
over meaningful rooftops.

It would all be easier than this

This care for my boy, girl
that I want to hold,
make safe, wrap around.

I do not know how.
I do not know how to feel,
carry a happy thought,
get its delicate bones home unbroken,
open a window of the possible
without cracking glass.

My father knew.
A wry smile,
a slight nod of approval.
That was love.

There was the summer
with his V6 car.
Its vast thigh of bench seat.
I sat in the middle.
My leg touched dad's
as he pressed the clutch.

Nylon on denim was enough.

Human Remains
For my father on his 90th birthday

When you read this, which you will not,
the last stanza will already be dark.

You will be a boy once more, in a nighttime of war.
In a scramble over broken brick,
inhalation of a Blitz of years,
the silted river,
dulled incendiary of your name.

You will be held again, in hormonal rush of flame
adolescent, intense
in the kick out of windows;
the crumbled, red stone terraces of an invisible city.

By the time you read this, which you will not,
what you are/were
will be worn as badge, notation.
Blood will be burnt.
The telephone you no longer answer will not be ringing.

A signpost with your name on it will not be read.
You will be faceless.

Darkness will have crept though your veins;
immaculate, wordless.

Suits will be worn, prayers said, flowers left.

We Came from Water

Part Two:

Words for My City

We Came from Water

Mapping the Dominion
New Westminster, 2016

3 a.m.
unseen rivers, in the leaky skiff of me
under elephantine, imperial skin,
a layer cake of brick.

The negotiation of words
over the underworld of lightless waters.

The darkened being of fish, sightlessness,
CAT Scan history,
every bone in our bodies revealed to the past.

Knife cuts on a shirtless back,
runes on tattooed arms,
the city singing itself whole,
in dementia recollection.

Believe this flesh.
It is the last known map of how it is.
Cosmopolitans in fear for their lives,
iPhones cowered under cut loose coordinates,
the monster headed fragments of empire
surrendered to multicultural,
its kill of infection,
the cross-cultural wheel ruts
to be followed towards fire and food;
the liberation in the maneuvering of tongues.

Spiderman on Sixth Street

My son's first skateboard is plastic.
It has Spiderman painted in flaky Day-Glo.

It is quite the compliment
that Spidey would want to ride this,
with these tiny tot wheels
that wedge into the sidewalk cracks.

It's a start, good for a month or so, if that.
In fact, I think both my son and I know
it may be nearer a week.

Yet that is ok.

We get the spider web kneepads,
a black and red helmet that is on sale.

We go for deep fried chicken, milkshakes,
sit in the restaurant window,
watch a bickering couple
in a parked Mercedes.

Their wheels; static, joyless.

We both know,
with their faces bent in anger,
these people will never save the world.

The Mirrored Bowl of Midnight
For the Sapperton District Taphouse

Out of bar light into night light, car lights
houselights of insomniacs, late show fanatics.

Cranked up on alcohol, divined by bend of bone
into alleyways, down dead ends
to run my feral tongue up the uncurled leg of Eighth Avenue;
lap the mirrored bowl of midnight.

I am swished with serotonin,
skin crinkled to the marinade of beer waves
that wash above my nose, blur the treetops,
clean me invisible, dress me in my best black,
whistle me past the police academy;
its antiseptic legal nosebag.

I step carefully past the empty cop cars
that stand cold, abandoned to disinterest;
victims of so much honesty, clarity.

Everyone is going somewhere good:
to visit family, old friends not seen for so many years,
a mother or father reconnected with, forgiven
or the ill, that have found themselves cured;
those that finally found God, gratefully lost him,
or a place where all marriages are to last,
children will live.

I am on to the backroads.

Five more minutes to home, ten to midnight.
Past the supermarket, the postal sorting office
where empty trucks stand ready
to be loaded with wanted news,
letters from the long lost, gifts that need to be given.

A History of New Westminster

First there is the history that will not, cannot, go away.

Genocide, murder, disease,
cancer beneath the beatific face,
rot in the centre of the bone,
colonial mission that was the bedrock
of all this hard work, enterprise
of this city from the afterbirth of ruin.

In its geometry of trade, odour of gold,
smallpox vapour trail, ice clot in the mind,
triplicate paperwork,
the immaculate copperplates of invading race
in the timber clear-cut for battleships,
scaffolding for Queen Victoria's conceits,
of progress marked on landscape in changeling smoke,
open wound, unreliable breath.

Branded in Old Testament, cauterised in the grope
of the poor, desperate,
of other continents, in ritual disembowelment
of forest, wilderness rationalized,
calculated in a count of beard lice
under winter sky,
crinoline sail tips of bride ships
in the grab, barter of newly delivered flesh
passing hand to hand
the unwanted wombs of old Europe
in the free market logic of symmetry, order
parks, municipal buildings, schools, brothels, barracks.

Then came people like me, industrial, working class
conceived in foundries, forges, infant factories
that made things, people realized they needed
believed they wanted:
engines, tractors, knife sharp machines, clothing,
medicines, if you squinted, held your breath,

We Came from Water

you could convince yourself had worth;
would bring prosperity, something for all.

In time, these things did mean something,
at least to us in our town, to people like us, our tribe
after World War II, nested between the Beatles,
the end of Vietnam.

After all that extravagance of world-wide death
came work for all that did or did not want it

when shoppers came again from valley farms
to marinate beneath bright lights,

country boys arrived to run their fingers
down the paintwork of the modern world;

each industry its own small universe
in sealed suburbs, downtown districts, social clubs,
theatres, marching bands.

When the hooters went,
the old Fords, Valiants
pumped themselves with purpose
up the stiff veins of gridded streets
back to the detached;
the snail shell curves, the chicane straights,
pristine crescents, avenues, perfected hedges,
purposeful garden ornaments ...

where everyone was richer than their dad has been.

Blues for the Penitentiary Dead

Square tags of stone, numbers, no names.
The prison is condos now.
Everything is condos.

These dead are all that's left.
No more will they go hungry, know pain.

My children
fight with umbrellas in belligerent spring rain,
skip between murderers, rapists,
the unwanted, unlucky.
The ones that just got caught.
Teen suicides, victims of accidents.

This is history
we do not know what to do with.

No more will they go hungry, know pain.

A strip of unwanted bodies
on the edge of a ravine
where there was once a stream,
now gone,
have been buried under concrete.

Here, there are these dead
we cannot bring ourselves to honour
or annihilate.

No more will they go hungry, know pain.

My Winter on Ewen Avenue

I am just above the river's edge in Queensborough,
custodian of the alluvial village built on water
on the best farmland there has ever been,
under a street built for a tram that isn't there
to connect across a bridge, where no passengers go.

An avenue with no big trees
painful to look at in its promise of future, community;
in its lack of yearling leaves.

It's eight months since my dad died.

I am here now on cheap land, place of immigrants
in financial, cultural exile, willed or unwilled isolation.

A wall of box stores wink
from beyond the open surgery of highway,
the wedged wide throat of traffic
that swallows the invisible, all conversation, history.

I ask directions
from a calm, clear senior in a battered suit
complete in his perfect Sudoku of immaculate turban
wrapped to pin the soil still, add a purpose to the air.

I walk down Wood Street
past family homes, rented basements,
minivans at the temple, where there is a meal.

Where there are white-tipped domes
under the approach to the Queensborough Bridge.
Where trucks take punches,
leave the ground as they gather up speed,
throw themselves, death defying, toward the city.

The Royal Columbian

Two places ahead, in the queue for emergency

the shackled junkie
twerks in filthy track pants, ill matched flip flops

convulses, dribbles
under the bruised eyes of the watchful cop.

In fact, everyone watches-
cautiously, as
silently as herbivores at a waterhole.

Yes,
the obligatory old person abandoned on a gurney

the usual teen suicide attempt
shivering, dwarfed in a hospital blanket

the multicultural collection of weepy children
with their broken fingers, concussion, asthma:

They all eye this blood-stained young man

who has already eaten through his own life
who is looking for others to devour.

Sandringham Avenue
New Westminster, 1911

Here there is an avenue with no trees.

These homes, for the poorer ones,
are scuttled at the bottom
of the long slide from Queens Park.

No royalty here, just a blue-collar safari,
wobbly eyed chicken, loose furred rabbit,
chiselled hemorrhoids of Edwardian woodwork,
untreated empire, tuberculosis for the flag,
the oil stained thumb of membership.

A map of varicose veins that has arrived in steerage,
uncushioned boards for eyes, chalkboard intestines.

School caned tramlines, beaten through forest,
back of the hands raised into the red welt of
Canada.

A wind chapped sunrise.

Loose tobacco smeared across the sky at sunset.

An unmoored spring evening clutched and rattled.

Christ-sized nails crucifying a blue jay sky.

Bleached canvas shucked among tree stumps.

Small children, armed with sticks,
mark out road grids in dirt,
city plans for a place that doesn't yet exist.

A girl on the back of a rickets wheeled wagon
mauls an out of tune piano into giving forth Chopin.

We Came from Water

Notes bounce off splintered stream heads;
invade, swarm a melody of an alien species.

The stubs of one-way tickets
are checked by a beaten breeze.
Thrown like confetti at a shotgun wedding.

An Englishman on 12th Street

I wait for my car repairs,
walk the military-made spine of 12th.Street
Its gridded exactness. Its sky, white as Queen Victoria's corsets.

This is where we came, colonized,
staked the edge of empire up this first road
in the interior, into all that jumble of hostile profit.

It's an uphill pull, past a bulge of used car lots,
skeletal factory sites birthing trench work,
umbilical powerlines of flowering condominiums

the Squat low-rise rental blocks, where people start or end up,
the young, new immigrants,
people negotiating their own brokenness,
the closed businesses, hopeful start ups.
Everything here is short-term; in transition.

By the Providence Orphanage site,
where the religious once cornered the lonely,
you see so many single men, heads steamed in anxiety,
a little too pale, skinny; on the edge of something, anything.

I am reminded
that when dad died, I held my hand under a candle.
I wanted pain, reality; just once to be allowed to cry.

An old lady outside the pizza joint
taps her feet to an unheard tune.
The year's first snow begins to fall.
Night curls its fingers to my throat.

We Came from Water

Paul McCartney
The New Westminster Years

Sunday morning in Glenbrook Ravine
in broken sports gear, yesterday's brand names,
running shoes with a gas victim wheeze.

This is where I worship. Here, no creep to the cross.
My faith, unmediated.
No socialites, hypocrites.

In my headphones, Paul, circa Let It Be.
His grey free beard, impractical fur coat.

He wobbles. Mud overwhelms his Cuban heels.

He struggles to keep up, spills his mug of tea
chatters on about Linda, his new love;
the vegetarian sausages
that will one day make him rich.

The sun is leaking, changeling, Lennon-faced.
It has spread its desire over a glittered brain
of dying leaves; a red, yellow, galaxy of rot.

Its rough thrown umbilical of death,
that snakes down,
circles at 33 and a third into the valley end.

It's just Paul and I,
here, in this unknown cut of land between condos,
the remnants of a federal prison site;
exercising in our hermitage,
this poor man's pocket paradise, escape route
in this happiness, collapse into oblivion;

'White Album' on repeat, one earbud each.

Cary Grant - 525 Sixth Street

He dropped his acid at the Hollywood Sanitarium,
525 Sixth Street, New Westminster, BC Canada;
now a strip mall where I buy my kids pizza.

He took drugs because his mother left him.

Every love he had, had been a way to get her back;
exact revenge.

Around here, amongst the insurance plans,
pensions of our well-nested suburbia,
he found joy, ecstasy, humanity.

Year by year,
I have found a slow retreat into silence, acceptance.

No, not the same,
but perhaps we all circle around
to a similar point in the end;
or at least there is a real possibility of that
if we live long enough. If life allows it.

A type of happy death, what we all would want.
I tell myself Cary had that.

This is what I want to believe
when I pick up the pepperoni, Hawaiian, the cheese;

in my life
where nothing much happens, again and again.

We Came from Water

New Westminster - Rock City

No cars without sex, sex without cars
without a well-paid job
at the foundry or pulp mill
where you were made to make your world;

given time under the foreman's heel
to clip together your own penis,
shape your own libido
into a recognizable dimension.

When you worked, you left it parked
in the half empty street
outside your parent's cold-water home,
beside their fist of cedar planking
where they had grown you,
in their home, a garden, skinny back yard
with tomatoes that winked from loam rich soil,
nuclear orange marigolds
pinned like medals on the smog jacketed sky.

Where your grandfather also lived;
who spoke no English,
who did wonders with string, rusted secateurs,
who on the sabbath at funerals,
sang songs from Ukraine, old Russia.

Untied old cloth, unpacked creased photos
of muscled farm horses,
a glittered disc of harvest moon,
stars taken from the Urals
that once hung above
silent homesteads of the imagination.

In Canada, outside in the empty street,
here was the proof
you could leave the past behind.

We Came from Water

A 1972 Mustang, engine uncurling like a tiger claw;
that lived to run its paws across the fabric of a Saturday night,
that had no other way to know exactly what it was.

You didn't need to dodge tanks or genocide here.

Not to get the girl, respect,
the confirmation that you were alive.

That came in the backseat fuck,
blow job in the IHOP carpark
with enough beer to float you through the sunroof,
inflate yourself upon the night,
unbutton yourself towards the Pacific,
wave it towards the Prairies.

That is why you queued for the bus,
Mondays at 6 a.m.
Became a peasant again
with all the other schmucks, meatheads;
broke your nails, sliced your knuckles,
lived in overalls, filthy clothes, leached oil,
fed the steel sheets into the press,
the logs into the saw.

Spoke to nobody; angry, alone,
foot paused over the pedal of a weekend yet to come.

Unpacked, those pictures in your head
of the tight jeaned girls that waited; wanted.

William Blake
237 Sandringham Avenue

I planted the apple tree.

Sliced
a fleshy slab of lawn.

Exposed
the many headed being of the soil
in the slip of shovel

between water mains, electric cables
that I prayed were not there.

Into unseeded earth,
rotten roots, matted into fists,
printed into the ground before suburbia.

Into the continents of bacteria,
undercover lungs,
in the citadels of worms,
the heavenly kingdom of the lowly
that I inched up to on my knees,
bent into
asked for a forgiveness
that was not to be given.

Swimming the Brunette

There was industry here once.
The empire grind of logging, milling, shipping.

Whey-faced children,
freshly sieved from *the old country*,
pressed their faces
to the heavy frame of titanic wooden windows.

Waited for overall-suited fathers
to deliver their wrought bodies home.

The mailman to skim in letters from aunts,
uncles that were never seen again.

Then history went backwards.
Nature unnaturally returned.

A municipal placed Eden, settled compactly
into a smooth administrative whisper
among the trees.

The many-headed highways, pythons of modernity
slumbered across the city's neck.

Here now, the post-industrial poor
yoke a scatter of rusted RVs into circles.

New immigrants shelter under ethnicity
picnic in an overload of summer.

A New Westminster

There were forests here once, a
deep pocket of a valley, the
limbs of a stream.

A crown of grazing cows.

A knife blade of
sunlight through high canopies,
its glint on slow turning fish.

We were goldpanners, woodsmen,
peasants of a disinterested empire.
Then later, labourers in foundries and mills
slipped into condom tight brick.

A little later again, shoppers,
occasionally someone's soldiers;
finally, voters, citizens.

Then it was gone; as if it had never been.

To leave us our shiny homes:
the same as our neighbors,
and *their* neighbors.
all those others whom we do not know.

The Arrival of My People
**"The *oppressed*, instead of striving for liberation,
tend themselves to *become oppressors*." ~ Paulo Freire**

England delivered me in blood, starch.
Tied me to apron strings of class, service
to do breaststroke in a royalty of afterbirth;
to corral me in a small holding of boyhood
subject, not citizen, uncrowned in my own land.

Plague land, plough land, animal Braille;
that place my ancestors had farmed.

My great uncle
had his stomach kicked out by a horse.

My great aunt, refugee from rat, rotted thatch -
whom the 1901 census proclaimed "madwoman" -
died hungry.

My great grandfather who groomed horses,
other people's, became cuffed to the village -
anywhere he could walk in one day -
as the self-appointed guard of village memory;
of a life of unions, machine breaking,
sharpened oaths, bloody scythes at midnight.

Under the penny-sized eyes of the squire;
the vampire cassock of the village priest.

My people lost their land.
The aristocracy, plotting rich, hid it all;
took it for themselves, behind walls, wire.

Their exile was Canada, poverty,
with the consolation of a chance to dream.
Imagine up new provinces, territories.
Push away the judges, the militia.
Clean the butcher's apron, the Union Jack.

We Came from Water

Tear the order of transportation,
hangman's directive, deeds of enclosure.

To polish up the copperplate of settlement
in the steal of one land for another.
The beginning of a country.
The story of it;
of how oppressed become oppressor
in the peg and slice of land, burnt eyes of forest.
In the leap from wagon to wagon,
lifeboat to lifeboat,
canoe to donkey back.

Over rivers, mountains, a continent,
taking what could be taken
until there was nowhere else to go.

A New Westminster was founded.

The Royal Visit
New Westminster, 1939

On Columbia Street, the medals are hard as gallstones.
King George, Queen Mary, open-topped, hatless,
heated on a griddle of unquestioned worship.

The rolls of re-used bunting, stretched one more time
from Queensborough to Queensland, Sapperton to Singapore.

They wave on automatic, to yet another crowd
to justify it all; all they have.

George says, "One day it will have to stop.
It is so tiring; all this waving to yourself."

He is being sandwiched
between the thick buttery smiles of motorcycle cops,
first growth gas tanks, Churchill wide tires.
The jangled trinkets of yesterday.
The municipal red brick of tomorrow.

Above the crowds he sees a river:
An old man fishing in a string vest
who glows in the sticky resin,
the thick cake of the wasp yellow sun.
A row of railway ties that twitch across this country
like old spinsters trying to nap.

He thinks about his long dead great grandmother
snoozing on a Balmoral Sunday.
The rattling crystal crowned by her snoring.

He sees the heavy husband of a locomotive,
that waits for him, buckles its gut,
stretches its tired limbs at the platform edge.

Empire Blues

See it there, with my wife's grandfather,
James Graham, arriving by train;
Canadian Pacific, 1923.

A Glaswegian city boy, knowing nothing and nobody.

See that he is seated in his allotted place, in third class.
Notice that he holds the roller-coasted grade.
Pockets the penny hard words -
power, elevation, sun, sky -
feels the worth of this new country.

He already knows its being
in the bone of steel and wood,
in the stanzas of vertical scree balanced over eye-sized lakes.

The permanence of smoke, fire hardened trestles,
burnt across a century, never quite burnt out.

He is a poor man with a hand full of syllables.
A future packed in his cardboard suitcase
of half understood verbs.
In his pocket-change coordinates,
a purse of unwritten letters.

Observe it:
His one palm pressed on a hernia
of half-digested history.
His other on a blank catalogue
not colour yet, still black and white.

Full of what has not happened.
Places, that for him, do not exist.

There Are Good People

In Starbucks, my one-year old son,
who I had been carting on my shoulders,
vomited a chicken curry on my head.

The afternoon spread itself before me like a pissed sheet.

Besides bile, animal bits in rivulets across my face,
the efficient staff that threw down traffic cones ...
what I remember is the silence.

Nobody laughed, as I would have done.

People carried on, stared intently into Frappuccinos,
dismembered chocolate chip cookies,
hurtled onwards into space,
towards love, death, the next meal.

This is what parenthood has taught me:

That there are better people than me.

To keep my children close,
keep their wreckage, human debris for my own;

That I will push on through the mess, regurgitation
half-thoughts, inadequacies of this existence
towards a meaning that may, or may not,
one day come to me,
isolated in front of strangers
watching me coolly wiping
whatever it is that has landed
on my shoes,
on the back of my jeans.

Karl Marx in Starbucks
Columbia Street, New Westminster

When he was in the queue,
being jostled by bored office drones,
the gentry held the land
still terrorized with their priests and lackeys.

By the time he had ordered
his triple macadamia pumpkin whip,
capital had come:

High finance, commerce
the shuffle of well-oiled lawyers.

Fact secreting professors
the form, the superstructure of it all
that he caught a flash of in the washroom mirrors.
In the old memories, personal enmities,
uniquely shaped sensations,
syntheses, antithesis.

Within the barricade storming, sugar rush illusions
in new modes of thought,
the shaping of his class in relation to others.
The forming of his hand around the paper cup.

In his thoughts,
that he himself was the actual motive;
the starting point of his own actions.

We Came from Water

The Hermit of Victory Heights

She collected candy wrappers as souvenirs.
Runes from the cities of old Europe.
Imported soft centres, hard planets,
essence of other places. Muscled sugar manifestoes
in a certainly of colours:

Vatican yellow, Enlightenment red,
Martin Luther pink, Alhambra blue,
a tinge of Stalin brown, Hitler black.

Each unwrapping, a delivery of centuries;
distilled, purified.

At first, she stored them in a shoebox,
then transported them to drawers;
threw away photos, books, to make room.

She filled the kitchen, lounge.
Eventually the bathroom, bedroom, gave way.
She slept on a hammock on the balcony
nested among crows, a weave of gypsy fiddle.
She lived outside of her own life.

Through the glass, another her served tea,
dished out bonbons, chocolate on fine china.
Served her smile on a platter of politeness,
finely glazed conversation.
Entertained the clever, the dead, intellectuals,
bohemians in lace and velvet:
Dostoevsky, Tolstoy, Camus.

She watched this better her
bed down in etiquette, tradition,
the puffed pillows of higher speech;
ease herself into the Morse of what could have been.

The River's Reach

Alcohol has always been me:
The warrior at evening's end,
The nurse of failed expectations.
The conjurer of silence, of a
oneness in numbness
a pure forgetfulness, a dismantling
in the completeness of vomit, sleep,
in the sanctity of bar glow
a lifelong dance with the crooked limbs
of a half-lit midnight

in the calm beneath the slur of verb,
bone free moment,
the float of my bloated self, expanded out,
raised into the air,
cut loose into a swim of deep,
a mouthful of blue beneath tables.

There is a totem line of cigarette butts,
a flood of party plans,
a grubby fingered hive of throbbing phones

runes of black shoe marks on hardwood floors,
communication of dot, dash, into deeper down,
into the sunk among ocean, garbage.

Outside the empty streets, mountains wait,
trackways curve away into interior, wilderness

where I will hide under pine,
lie under hedgerows;
to be held in the fist of innocence
in perpetual summer; for nothing,
everything,
in all life, death, at once.

Woodlands Hospital, 1963

The solidity of sound.
The open jaws of the air take me in their teeth,
swallow stars of ice.

A silence
folded suburbia back into its own pocket.

Pressed it into the open palm of a whiteness,
into a swirl of prefabricated space,
double doors.

Held itself
to the iron, imperial, heartbeat of starched linen.

At a window, a young woman of 18 or 19
emotionally arthritic,
Bipolar, crabbed into a child's plastic chair.

She is to wait for ECT.
Pinched between her fingers is a coffee
gone cold.

In her eyes, four seasons
being restrained beneath an avalanche.

The Commonwealth Blues

I am a fake, an import, hiding
between countries

caught in traffic at the city's edge:
between fender benders, tantrums,
on the Queensborough bridge,

caught between the jaws of heavy trucks,
a thousand mini malls.

I am a new immigrant in hiding
between the mountains, the Pacific.

North of here
there is a Canada of a thousand languages,
Aboriginal cultures, histories, that
have no need for me

That is the way it must be
I am here, invader on their land

They will not be made to speak.

Going Home, Queensborough 1948

In the morning I worked on my cousin's boat
to catch logs, debris, drag them to the shore.
Acres of broken homes, fences, dead cows.

In the afternoon, sandbagged the Queensborough Dyke.
Not more than two people wide, inadequate

Worked with the army.
A man, with a wooden leg,
called *Scotty,* up from Mississippi
taught us how to plug a leak.

Seven hundred carried sand, shovels.

Sometimes I was the sky, then the earth.
I did not know where I ended, the river began;
what I was, which element.

I choose land instead of water, death.

I was young then, a few years back from the war;
head still full of D-Day, purpose.

In the evening I went home.
My furniture had been swept away; family gone.
Just the kitchen table left,
where my six-month son had lain all day.
Untouched, abandoned in my empty house.
Somehow, left alive; one smile away from laughter.

I could not be sure anymore
what he was, whose work he did;
exiled, apart from us, a cold-water Moses,
infantile Neptune, passenger, maybe God
at the cross point into the world of fish.

We Came from Water

Beyond Us, the End of the West

On the promenade
the ocean cracks its head on concrete.

Every moment, a perpetual death, birth;
boxy stores of sickly light hawk postcards
nobody will ever buy.
Ice cream, water wings out of season.

An alien blue dinghy hangs on a gibbet.
A panicked breeze scatters itself.

At the legion, meat raffles,
a fat rack of wheelchairs.

A thin man in a dirty jacket mauls an accordion,
serenades a pint of beer
the colour of a forgotten penny.

Outside, nose to the sidewalk, a crumpled parent.
Her unleashed children, sniff out sugar,
shiny plastic.

A roost of teenage girls
impersonate the middle-aged.

By the thrift store,
a swollen lip of refugees, turned inward
on a tide of Arabic, stand
by elephantine suitcases.

Bright white price tags flap in surrender,
powerlessness.

A muzzle of fattened SUVs spreads, invades,
slobbers across every available space.

Inland from the town, there is another country.

We Came from Water

The dark-eyed fields split their limbs;
manicure their immaculate, bank manager fingers
allocate the symmetry of wall, ditch.

Cows are led to barns. Blinds drawn down.
Rooms tidied, made complete, ready for night;
held for inspection, like the face of a woman
I once loved, who I thought I had forgotten.

We Came from Water

A Hymn for My City

I am home, in evolutionary grip of chimp,
swim of fish, in adjustment of tie, sliver from the swamp.

O Canada, my home and native land.
O Canada, killer, protector in all measure.
O Canada, with the Janus face.
O Canada, with a latte, switchblade in your hand.

I am home in firelight,
Ethiopian cave mouth, primordial Nordic forest,
Indus river valley, as occasional stitch
in the hem of heaven.

I know it, accept it, a mouth full
of cold soil, the finality of my own gleaming skull
in infinite line of other planets,
raised bump from Newton's apple,
when I ride a motorbike
around the walls of my empty head.

O Canada, my home and native land.
O Canada, killer, protector in all measure.
O Canada, with the Janus face.
O Canada, with a latte, switchblade in your hand.

Home is the sturgeon in my blood, whale-headed,
yesterday, comfortless past of spilt blood, hate,
reality of our indigenous genocide,
memory of those slaughtered
for our place on the couch, a car in the drive.

Home is when we ask them back,
to eat, drink;

We Came from Water

when we insist the dead
warm themselves with the living.

O Canada, my home and native land.
O Canada, killer, protector in all measure.
O Canada, with the Janus face.
O Canada, with a latte, switchblade in your hand.

Home is those unknown cousins, aunts, uncles
in places we have never been;
in how they play, gossip,
conjure laughter from the dark.

We Came from Water

Part Three:

Words for My Wife

We Came from Water

Let Us Eat Cake
for Frances

All afternoon, your sister baked you cake.

A four-layered megalith,
elephantine babel of chocolate
as décadent as Marie Antoinette,
pure as Eden before that apple thing.

A lava of coffee glaze that burst over the lip of the plate,
threatened to engulf villages,
sweep away huddled groups of diabetics praying for mercy.

Our children daubed themselves,
took spears, hunted the mailman.
The economy of the Caribbean took a boost.

This is how your birthday should always be.

Sugar seduced us, rolled us,
threw our clothes from an open window;
left us naked
to climb down a mountain
of high cholesterol at 1 a.m.

In my one hand a plate, in yours a fork:
We are armed. We are family coming for you,
ready to fight.

Saigon East Vancouver
For My Wife

In her first years
it was thrift store clothing,
her family's no-food bank pride,
low rise rental,
mid-seventies desolation chic,
bedded in blue-collar varicose basement reds,
psychedelic drapes.

A mandala of cigarette burns along
a Nixon era sofa.

A heavy freight line,
fished past the toothy back fence,
train-shaken windows,
frames wedged shut with prayer.

This was slum land fashion.
The poverty permanent as moonlight;
temporary as tenancy.

A bare wire shock, faulty socket in the brain.
A highway edged rice paddy of blood.
Somewhere. Never.

A fly-tipped, thin, new motherland.
Life in plastic bags. Accumulated discounts.

Here, the first days of a small child's
new way of being, new continent.

Always one minute to midnight;
too many to payday.
A loose front door
the only defence against a city.

Pizza
for Frances

In the living room, Saigon fell.

Mum called from the kitchen;
the pizza was ready.

Somewhere,
in the Republic of South Vietnam,
my future mother-in-law
wept in terror by a radio.

The seed of my unborn wife
lay camouflaged within her.

Her army had fled.
A scat of rifles, helmets, discarded uniforms
dammed Highway Number One.

Hot cheese burnt the roof of my mouth.

My schoolbag, jacket
lay abandoned by the back door.

Spring
tipped itself in from high windows.
A stunted apple tree
squirmed against the glass.

Helicopters threw themselves
into the Pacific.
People huddled
on an embassy roof.

The cat pressed the back of my leg
begged for food.

Fairy Tale

That fat thing at the end of your bed.

It is me.

How tolerant you are
in your beauty;
that I am too full of pills to rise to.

Five years you slept.

What awoke you, even you do not know.

Your voodoo head shrinker with the Mercedes
cannot tell you.

I do not ask.
I am amazed I am here;
that you have returned to me.

You, so surprised to be back;
that it was my kiss, not some other's,
that brought you home again.

I am what I am, always was,
a frog.

Within you, something shifted;
a rock, straw from a camel's back;
my foot from your toe.

I am still here; adequate, inadequate,
almost yours.

Recital

In the next room she plays alone.
My wife,
with a nylon stringed guitar.

When she was a child
it was her Mother who made her learn
the consistency of music
as they moved
basement suite to basement;
their poverty a melody of repetition,
refrain.

There were slaps, kicks for talking back,
shouts if she did not practice;
or if she did.

Such beauty,
so dependent on coercion, violence.

Now she plays at night
when nobody can hear.
Each note now hers.

Her calloused fingertips,
the medals she wears
for nobody.

Heat Wave

Every window forced open,
a tired breeze stretchered in
on the back of a July night.

How long it had been since rain.

The garden stained by drought
lay quiet.

My wife and I
ferried bath water out to the flowers,
baptised the hydrangeas in our soap dirt.

It was all we could offer them.
There was nothing else.

Life needed us,
had included us in its own reflection.

That night we made love.

The first time in months.

Wedding Night

Your smile, its flooded canal
tipped into my mouth, drowned me
in the rise, swell of candlelit bedroom,
tangle of gaseous, disco shaken garlands,
lei of plastic flowers, willing dissipation.

I heard your call,
as the night collapsed,
folded its knees
in a machine gun pop, pull of buttons,
an insistent swish,
navigation of cold hands on warm flesh;
the close and lock of every door of us.

A full magazine of gold cufflinks
emptied itself on to polished pine floorboard;
torpedoed midnight moaned,
pushed its feet up, held up the moon.

Our love was high windows,
Victorian plasterwork floated on laughter,
double doors broken open onto grassy darkness,
cracked glass that framed,
those warning lights for low flying aircraft,
pinned as medals
against black mountain tops.

Minotaur

Between us, my wife and I,
there is this being that will not be killed.

Monster, familiar, confident, realtor of all flesh.

It has no interest in reason.
It flicks its lighted matches
into the darkened room of us;
illuminates the flab, fold,
the crumpled manifesto of what we were to be;
can, sometimes, still be.

It feeds on us with its immeasurable body
in the cut of shadows, torn gown of doubt.

It hunts in the labyrinth of caves,
tunnels beyond the conscious tip
of all we know of it
to bellow in its bull-sized being
in every slight caress
against the press of flesh;
the leaky ship of us.

At night, this creature comes to track me down.

However fearful I may be
I let its jaws close on my neck, crush me, pull me in.

Let the pain of my dissolution, defeat
become us; be us.

Marriage Guidance

We started with the obvious:

What five things do you like about your mother? I mine?

What do you value most in a partner?

What have been your five top happiest experiences?

Then, as the embarrassment set itself over us
there were the questions we added for ourselves:

What would you choose to have - a robotic arm or a robotic leg?

What are your five favorite candy bars?

What top six celebrity chefs would you want to French kiss?

How far would we get if we tried to hop up Mount Everest?

Then the questions I wanted to ask, but could not:

What top five ways will it hurt me
to know you no longer love me?

In how many places will I break
when the avalanche of your disappearance rolls over me?

Fireworks

At one time we still touched:

expressed our love
through contact,
offer of our unbothered bodies.

through
the effortlessness of being young.

Before children, mortgages,
the slackening of flesh
left me to distrust what the mirror
had to give to me,
left me to want cover, darkness.

There will always be Hanoi.

That place of your mother's enemies
where I woke you
to watch fireworks,
naked on the roof.

The city, with its shadow gone,
unfolded out below us
in its silken sheet,
and in the brief brilliance
of that a moment
wrapped us in its life.

Where We Live

After thirteen years, we don't have it;

The animal shift between bodies, minds,
tide divined, atom frigged copulations.
The tawdry pose, empty squeak
of ready flesh.
Happy shopper, money back guarantee.
Cosmo love.

What we have are stretch marks,
maps, runes, scars;
ruts we have become.

The cracked elastic of your kiss.

An accumulation of tiny stones of kindness
that have become a cairn;
a wall against a tide of unsaid words.

Then the knowing, planned surrenders,
treaties we have made against oblivion.

Temporary, but enough proof;
we are no longer tourists
that this is where we live.

We Came from Water

Author Profile

Alan Hill is the 4th Poet Laureate of the City of New Westminster and President of the Royal City Literary Arts Society. Alan is the Past President of the Royal City Literary Arts Society He has published four collections of poetry in addition to being published in over forty literary magazines and periodicals across Europe and North America.

We Came from Water

www.ingramcontent.com/pod-product-compliance
Lightning Source LLC
Chambersburg PA
CBHW062148100526
44589CB00014B/1729